Sports Law in Turkey

Sports Law in Turkey

Third Edition

Anil Gürsoy Artan

This book was originally published as a monograph in the International Encyclopaedia of Laws/Sports Law.

Founding Editor: Roger Blanpain
General Editor: Frank Hendrickx
Volume Editor: Michele Colucci

Wolters Kluwer

Published by:
Kluwer Law International B.V.
PO Box 316
2400 AH Alphen aan den Rijn
The Netherlands
E-mail: lrs-sales@wolterskluwer.com
Website: www.wolterskluwer.com/en/solutions/kluwerlawinternational

Sold and distributed by:
Wolters Kluwer Legal & Regulatory U.S.
920 Links Avenue
Landisville, PA 17538
United States of America
E-mail: customer.service@wolterskluwer.com

ISBN 978-94-035-3638-5

e-Book: ISBN 978-94-035-3648-4
web-PDF: ISBN 978-94-035-3658-3

The Author

Anıl Gürsoy Artan was born in Ankara, Turkey, on 15 January 1978. She received her Law degree from Ankara University, School of Law in 2002. She did her Master's in International Sports Law at ISDE–IEB in Madrid in 2007. She is a member of the Ankara Bar Association.

After working for four and a half years for the Turkish Football Federation as an in-house legal counsellor, between October 2008 and December 2014, she worked as a partner at Yogurtcuoglu & Gürsoy Attorneys-at-Law. As of December 2014, she works as a sole practitioner.

The Author

Table of Contents

List of Abbreviations

CAS	Court of Arbitration for Sport
ECJ	European Court of Justice
EU	European Union
FC	Football Club
FDC	FIFA Disciplinary Code
FIFA	*Fédération Internationale de Football Association* (International Federation of Association Football)
IAAF	International Association of Athletics Federation
IOC	International Olympic Committee
ITL	Income Tax Law
RFEF	*Real Federación Española de Fútbol* (Royal Spanish Football Federation)
TFF	*Türkiye Futbol Federasyonu* (Turkish Football Federation)
TUMOK	*Türkiye Milli Olimpiyat Komitesi* (Turkish National Olympic Committee)
UEFA	*Union des Associations Européennes de Football* (Union of European Football Associations)
UNESCO	United Nations Educational, Scientific and Cultural Organization
VAT	Value Added Tax
WADA	World Anti-doping Agency

List of Abbreviations

Acknowledgements

When I first wrote this monograph in the year 2008, I defined 'sports law' as a new branch of Law in Turkey. However, it has been sixteen years since and now sports law is a rising star among new colleagues. The number of practitioners is increasing day by day, but unfortunately, we still have limited 'quality' sources in Turkish academic literature. I hope this study would be of help for those who are interested to learn about Turkish Sports Law. I would like to thank all my friends, colleagues and professors from the Law School and Master's programme.

I would also like to thank my parents for their endless support, my husband for his love and being my best friend for all these years, and finally my darling son for his endless energy and unconditional love.

Rize, 31 March 2024
Anıl Gürsoy Artan

Acknowledgements

General Introduction

Chapter 1. General Background

1. One could expect more people would be practising sports professionally when one hears about a country of over 85 million people. However, with its 40% young population, Turkey is still below expectations.

As it is widely accepted by the community, sports is just a hobby and should stay as a hobby. Most of the parents encourage their children to pursue education and go to university rather than take up sports as a profession. This common understanding is borne from the fact that only a minority of the sportsmen's level of income is at an acceptable amount. The chain reaction begins with this fact; fewer people take up sports as profession, so the law follows them with the same small steps.

Since football is the most popular sports in Turkey, it is also the most legally advanced branch of sports law. Basketball, volleyball and handball follow football in team sports. The numbers are getting dramatically low when it comes to individual sports.

In order to raise both the number of sportsmen and interest in sports, the government should invest more in sports and take precautions in the education system to prevent children from giving up choosing sports for their higher education.

I believe that when sports is widely practised by people and interest in sports increases eventually, the law will evolve.

Today, sports law is just an elective course in some of the law schools in Turkey, but the upsurge of interest in sports law is encouraging.

Chapter 2. Sources of Sports Law

§1. Historical and Legislative Development of Sports Law

2. On 14 July 1922, sixteen clubs united and formed the 'Turkish Training Associations Union' to ensure the practice of sports under discipline. This Union, having the nature of a legal person, had the duty to represent the Turkish sports.

3. In the following years, the Union changed its name to 'Turkish Sports Organization' and moved its headquarters to Ankara, the capital.

4. On 29 June 1938, with Law No. 3530, General Directorate of Physical Education was established. With this law, the General Directorate was directly under the supervision of the Prime Minister, but in 1942, the Directorate was reorganized and from then on was moved under the supervision of the Ministry of Education. In 1969, the Ministry of Youth and Sports was established, and since then the Directorate was moved under this new Ministry's supervision. In 1983, the General Directorate was again moved under the Ministry of Education, Youth and Sports. Finally, in 1989, 'Education' and 'Youth and Sports' were divided, and Youth and Sports moved under the supervision of Ministry of State. On 24 January 1989, the name of the General Directorate was changed to 'General Directorate of Youth and Sports'. On 8 June 2011, with Decree Law (Executive Order) No. 638 published on the Official Bulletin, the Ministry of Youth and Sports was established. Today, all the sporting organizations and events are under the authority of this Ministry.

5. In 1993, after the autonomy of the Turkish Football Federation (TFF) was recognized, other sports federations' autonomy period had also begun. Before 1993, the presidents of the federations were appointed by the Minister of Youth and Sports. The first elections were held on 5 December 1993.

6. With the new Law on Sports Clubs and Federations No 7405, which was enacted in 2022, the procedures and requirements on the establishment of sports clubs, joint-stock companies of sports and also sports federations have been reformed.

7. Detailed information about the sports federation and legislation thereof will be discussed under further topics.

8. Sports Law finds its place in Articles 58 and 59 of the Constitution.

§2. Youth and Sport

I. Protection of the Youth

9. Article 58 – The state shall take measures to ensure the training and development of the youth into whose keeping our state, independence and our Republic are entrusted, in the light of the contemporary science, in line with the principles and reforms of Ataturk, and in opposition to ideas aiming at the destruction of the indivisible integrity of the state with its territory and nation.

The state shall take necessary measures to protect the youth from addiction to alcohol, drug addiction, crime, gambling and similar vices and ignorance.

II. Development of Sports and Arbitration

10. Article 59 – The state shall take measures to develop the physical and mental health of Turkish citizen of all ages and encourage the spread of sports among masses.

The state shall protect successful athletes.

The decisions of the sports federations regarding the administration of the sports or its disciplinary proceedings shall only be appealed to mandatory arbitration. The decisions of this mandatory appeals committee are final and binding; these decisions shall not be appealed to any other courts of law.

11. All the sports activities are supervised under the Ministry of Youth and Sports.

12. Law No. 3289 Law on Youth and Sports Services regulates the administrative structure of the Ministry.

13. Law No. 5894 is named as Law on the Establishment and Duties of the TFF. It is one of the rare examples in football that the federation is being established by law. Detailed information will be given under Part I Chapter 1 *infra*.

14. Law No. 7405 Law on Sport Clubs and Sport Federations has been enacted in the year 2022 and has already been revised in the year 2023. Article 1 of the Law is self-explanatory:

> Purpose and Scope
>
> ARTICLE 1 – (1) This law aims to define and outline procedures and requirements on the establishment of sport clubs, joint-stock companies for sports, and also sports federations and their bodies, and establishment of supervising organizations. This Law also states and underlines terms and conditions on their income and expenses, budget and expenditure principles as well as their duties, authorities and responsibilities, and auditing procedures. Another aspect of this Law is to regulate the procedures and principles regarding the form and conditions of all kinds of assistance that shall be provided to them and other issues related to them … .

15. Law No. 6222 is named as Law Regarding the Prevention of Violence and Disorderliness in Sports. Detailed information will be given under Part I Chapter 2 *infra.*

Part I. Organization of Sports

Chapter 1. Sports Governance

§1. Governmental Institutions and Bodies: Ministry of Youth and Sports

I. Legal Nature

16. The Ministry of Youth and Sports is a public body. All the transactions of the Ministry are subject to administrative law.

17. All the stadiums or any other movable or immovable properties relating to sports are owned by the Ministry of Youth and Sports.

II. Functioning

18. The Ministry functions in central and provincial organizations.

19. The central organization is composed of several service units and organized under 'General Directorates'. The General Directorates are: Sports Services, Credits and Dormitories, Investment and Operations, International Organizations and Foreign Relations, Legal Services, Strategy Development, Education Research and Coordination, Youth Services, Personnel, Information Technologies, Social Relations and Communication, Support Services.

§2. Sports Federations

20. Sports federations have been regulated under Law No. 7405.

21. There are sixty-four sports federations. Apart from the olympic and paralympic sports federations, there are a few federations which cannot be categorized, i.e., traditional sports federation, sports for all federation, e-sports, etc.

I. Sports Federations

22. At Law No. 7405, Law on Sports Clubs and Sports Federations, the definition of a sport federation has been defined under Article 2 as follows:

> n) Sports federation: refers to the federations that are established by law or Presidential decree to carry out activities related to sports. Managing bodies of these federations are elected to be entitled as on duty, and they have administrative and financial autonomy.

23. Part Three of the above-mentioned Law is dedicated to sports federations (except TFF). According to Article 26 of Law No. 7405, sports federations are established by or Presidential decree to carry our activities related to the sports branch, and they become legal entities upon publication of the law or decree of establishment in the Official Gazette.

24. Additional Article 9 and 9A of Law No. 3289 widely regulates how a federation establishes its bodies and the procedures of establishment. Below, you may find the translation of important parts of the said article:[1]

> The Appeals Committee is composed of seven members and seven substitute members. The five of the seven members shall be lawyers and remaining two members shall be scholar, manager or technical director in sports world. The members are appointed by the Ministry of Youth and Sports for four years. Judges and public prosecutors and those deemed to be of this profession may take office in the Appeals Committee by taking into consideration the principles of the guarantee of judgeship and by obtaining the approval of the authorised boards. The members choose a president among themselves. The decisions taken by the Appeals Committee is final.
>
> The Appeals Committee examines and renders the final decisions upon the appeals lodged by the related parties on the decisions of the Executive Committee of the federations with respect to the disputes arises between Federation and clubs, the Federation and referees, the Federation and technical directors and coaches, clubs and technical directors, coaches, and players, clubs and clubs and the appeals lodged against the decisions of the Disciplinary Committees. The Appeals Committee shall examine and finalize the disputes between the Ministry of Youth and Sports and the federations and the federations themselves upon objection.
>
> The Appeals Committee decides upon the objection of those concerned against the decisions to be taken by the Central Sports Disciplinary Committee as a result of the referral to the Central Sports Disciplinary Committee by the Ministry of Youth and Sports in the event that the president of the federation

1. Several parts of the below given Article have been annulled by the Constitutional Court's decision number E.2006/118, K.2009/107 dated 2 Jul. 2009. The information regarding the said decision will be given under para. 23.

and the members of the management, disciplinary and supervisory boards are found to have acted contrary to sports ethics and discipline.

The Appeals Committee shall be independent and impartial in its duties. Unless the members resign or are deemed to have withdrawn, no new members may be appointed in their place. The Appeals Committee shall not appoint a new member unless he/she resigns or is deemed to have resigned. The Appeals Committee shall not appoint a new member unless he/she has been sentenced to a ban for six months at a time or one year in total within the last five years by the sports disciplinary committees of the Ministry, the disciplinary committees of national or international sports federations, or has been sentenced to imprisonment for one year or more for an offence committed deliberately, or has been pardoned; Crimes against the security of the state, crimes against the constitutional order and the functioning of this order, embezzlement, extortion, bribery, theft, fraud, forgery, abuse of trust, fraudulent bankruptcy, bid rigging, bid rigging, bid rigging, laundering of assets derived from crime, financing of terrorism, smuggling, hatred and discrimination, crimes against sexual immunity, prostitution, manufacture and trade of drugs or stimulants, Those who have been convicted of the offences of facilitating the use of drugs or stimulants, purchasing, accepting or possessing drugs or stimulants for use or using drugs or stimulants, match-fixing or incentive premium, illegally playing betting and games of chance based on sports competitions, providing a place and opportunity for them to be played, advertising them, mediating the transfer of money or violating Article 20 of the Law on Sports Clubs and Sports Federations cannot be members of the Appeals Committee.

25. The Appeals Committee, which is mentioned in the article, is one of the units in the General Directorate organization. It makes it impossible to name the Appeals Committee as an independent body. All the sports federations, except football federation, are under the jurisdiction of the same Appeals Committee.

II. Operation of a Federation

26. Headquarters of all sports federations are in Ankara. The central organization of sports federations consists of general assembly, management, audit, disciplinary boards and general secretariat. The main status of the newly established sports federations is prepared by the Ministry.

27. The general assembly is the supreme part of the sports federation. All kinds of transactions related to the convening of the general assembly are carried out by the board of directors. The general assemblies of sports federations are held in Ankara.

28. The Ministry shall appoint persons in charge of surveillance in general assembly meetings. Such a person checks whether the general assembly meeting is held in accordance with the legislation and submits his report to the Ministry within fifteen days. The Ministry and those concerned may request the annulment of the general assembly in the Ankara Civil Court of First Instance within thirty days from the date of the general assembly.

29. At the General Assembly Meetings, the basic procedures and principles regarding the meeting of the board, determination of the delegates, formation of the council, objections to the delegate list, creation of the candidate lists of the management, audit and disciplinary committees, holding the elections and counting the votes are determined by the regulation to be issued by the Ministry, and other matters are determined by the main statute.

30. The number of general assembly delegates shall not be less than 150 or more than 300 in Olympic and Paralympic sports, and it cannot be less than 100 or more than 200 in other branches.

31. Ordinary general assembly: shall be held within three months from the end of the relevant Olympic Games in Olympic and Paralympic sports branches, summer Olympic Games in other sports branches, and the date of publication of the decision in the Official Gazette in the newly established sports federations.

32. Extraordinary General Assembly may convene:

(a) The decision of the majority of the total number of members of the sports federation board of directors.
(b) Written application of the majority of the delegates in the last general assembly meeting through the notary public.
(c) Resignation of the president of the Federation, loss or death of any of the conditions for becoming the president.
(ç) In the event that the number of members of the management or disciplinary board falls below the quorum of the meeting, it shall be carried out in case of any of these situations.
(d) Only the members of the disciplinary board shall be elected in the extraordinary general assembly to be held due to the decrease in the number of the members of the disciplinary board to the quorum of the meeting.
(e) Financial general assembly shall be held on the date specified in the status once every two years.
(f) In cases not released in the financial general assembly or specified in the fifth paragraph of this article, an elected extraordinary general assembly shall be convened within sixty days at the latest to elect a new board of directors to complete the remaining period instead of the president and board members. In the event that the president of the Federation loses any of the conditions for being president, this period starts from the finalization of the decision. However, in the cases specified in subparagraphs (b) and (c) of the fifth paragraph, an extraordinary general assembly may not be held until six months have elapsed from the date of the last meeting or if there is less than six months left before the Olympic Games are held in the Olympic and Paralympic sports branches.

Sports federation employees cannot be delegates of the general assembly. The number of delegates of the clubs in the general assembly may not be less than 60% of the total number of delegates. Ten percent of the number of delegates of the general assembly consists of Ministry delegates.

33. The mandatory organs of a sports federation are the Board of Directors, Disciplinary Board, and Audit Board. Apart from the mandatory organs, a Sports Federation may establish other boards that are necessary for their operation.

34. 'General Secretariat' is also a mandatory office to be established by Law No. 7405.

35. Incomes of a sports federation are defined under Article 39. The incomes are: shares allocated from the budget of the Ministry, resources transferred from the budget of the Ministry to support the projects related to the improvement of education and infrastructure, contribution fees, application fees and dues, visa fees and attributed shares from the transfer of coaches, referees and athletes, collection of registration fees of clubs, collection of accumulated revenues that shall be obtained broadcasting, revenues to be obtained from economic enterprises established in relation to sports branches within the scope of duty of education, course, seminar and sports federation, sponsorship, revenues from advertisements, printed publications and printed documents, revenues over penalties and indemnities by appeal, financial contributions and donations, rents and income generated from facilities, application fees received from the presidential candidates of the Federation and other similar income.

36. The properties of sports federations are considered to be State property and cannot be seized. The requests regarding the seizure of the sports federation's properties are rejected by the execution offices.

37. The Ministry has the power to inspect, audit and investigate a sports federation. Any type of inconvenience or loss that would be identified as a result of the inspection carried out by the Ministry shall be indemnified from the relevant persons. This indemnification shall be requested by the Ministry. Even though sports federation board is declared as discharged from debts by the general assembly, this clearance shall not exempt the board of directors from the responsibility that might arise as a result of the audit. The scope of the Ministry inspection to be carried out in terms of sports federations that have their own founding law shall be limited until the extent that all in-kind and cash contributions to be made by the Ministry are limited to the determination of the spending and use of the allocations in accordance with the legislation and purpose. Any type of financial inconvenience or losses determined as a result of the audit shall be indemnified by the relevant persons by the Ministry. The release of the sports federation board, which has its own establishment law (i.e., TFF), by the general assembly does not eliminate the responsibility of the board of directors as a result of the audit. Regarding crimes or misfits committed, those who are in charge of the activities of the Federation are considered to be public officials, where it is deemed to be an aggravating circumstance in the Criminal Code.

38. The expenditure principles are also defined under Article 43, where sports federations are not allowed to borrow more than 10% of the preceding year's income. Moreover, the president and members of the sports federation are jointly and severally responsible for any type of financial losses or inconvenience that may occur if they violate their obligations arising from the legislation intentionally or negligently. However, no intention or negligence is sought in the responsibilities of those who cause damage in case of violation of this paragraph. In this case, the sports federation and its creditors can directly follow up those responsible for the amount charged to the sports federation.

39. The supervision and inspection power of the Ministry and the right to appoint 10% of the general assembly delegates of a sports federation by the Ministry are question marks on the 'autonomy'. With these authorities, the government without a doubt interferes in sports administration.

III. Turkish Football Federation

40. Since football is the most common sports branch in Turkey, it has developed in a short period of time, in its both legal structure and economy. Therefore, in this chapter, TFF will be explained in detail.

A. A Brief History

41. It is known that the game of football was first played in the last quarter of the nineteenth century in Turkey. It all started in Thessaloniki during the Ottoman period and spread down to the meadows of Bornova. The first football club (FC) was formed by a group of English people in Izmir. Spreading further to Istanbul and being played in the meadows of Kadikoy and Moda, the fever for football managed to attract the attention of almost all the cities. The first match played between the Izmir selection and the Istanbul selection in 1897 was recorded as the first football match ever played on the Turkish territory.

42. Following the formation of the Union of Turkish Training Associations, being Turkey's first sports authority, TFF was established under the name 'Futbol Hey'et-i Muttehidesi' in 1923, and Yusuf Ziya Onis was elected as the first President. Following the Federation's establishment, Turkey applied to the International Federation of Association Football (FIFA) for membership and became FIFA's twenty-sixth member on 21 May 1923.

43. As a FIFA member, the Turkish National Team played its first international match against Romania at the Istanbul Taksim Stadium on 26 October 1923, only three days before Turkey was declared a republic and became the Republic of Turkey.

44. During that period until 1936, the first Turkish Championship was held in Ankara.

45. Along with the revocation of the Turkish Sports Agency in 1938 and placement of Turkish sports under the rule of the General Directorate of Physical Training, the state started to govern football.

46. The milestones of Turkish football between 1950 and 1960 were as follows: the professional football leagues were formed in Istanbul, Ankara and Izmir; the number of FCs in other cities rapidly increased; Galatasaray, Goztepe and Fenerbahçe achieved successful results in European cups; and foreign players started to play for Turkish clubs. In 1962, the Union of European Football Associations (UEFA) declared Turkey's full membership.

47. TFF started to organize 'Turkish Cup' in the 1962–1963 seasons for Turkish clubs to qualify for the UEFA Cup Winners' Cup. Additionally, in 1967, the twentieth European U-21 Football Championship was hosted by Turkey.

48. The 1970s witnessed an 'Anatolian Revolution' in Turkish football. Trabzonspor achieved the championship title in just its second year in the Turkish League, upon which it was promoted in 1974. Trabzonspor achieved a total of six league championships in a short period of time and played a leading role in football's spread across Anatolia.

49. In the 1980s, though the approach to club management changed, no important changes in the level of football played were witnessed, except for a few successful results. Galatasaray played in the semi-finals of the European Champions Cup in the late 1980s.

50. In the same period, Senes Erzik was appointed President of TFF with the support of Turgut Özal, the then Prime Minister of Turkey, in 1989, and the appointment of Mr Erzik has been a milestone in Turkish football history. During his presidency, infrastructural programmes were given priority and systematic training conditions were created. Turkish football took a series of initiatives and made revolutionary decisions in the 1990s. In 1990, Mr Erzik was elected by the UEFA Congress to UEFA's Executive Committee as the first Turkish delegate and later appointed as vice-president of two major Committees. All the infrastructural investments made paid off in 1992, and Turkey's U-19 National Team achieved its first European Championship title. The successful results, such as the European Championships achieved in 1994 and 2005, obtained in the following years proved that the first European Championship title was not by chance.

51. TFF earned autonomy in 1992. The developments and changes in football showed that it was more than a sport. The financial values increasingly created by football and the widening interest in football showed that football had to be governed by an autonomous organization. Law No. 3813, adopted on 17 June 1992, granted autonomy to TFF. Pursuant to Article 1 of the Law:

> the Turkish Football Federation was established as an autonomous organization and as being subject to private law for the purposes of conducting and organizing football activities in line with national and international rules and representing Turkey in and outside Turkey in the field of football.

52. The centralized broadcasting system, which was introduced in 1997, helped clubs generate broadcasting revenues in hundreds of millions of US Dollars. The successful results obtained, particularly those of the National Team, in the following years paved the path towards sponsorship and helped TFF sign huge agreements, providing added value of millions of US Dollars to the Turkish football economy. The importance of football economy was also realized by club managements, which later signed sponsorship agreements.

53. The year 1993 was also an active year for TFF. TFF hosted U-16 European Championship and introduced the Fair Play principle in the Turkish Leagues. Also, the anti-doping programmes implemented in the same year paid off well. TFF President Senes Erzik was elected UEFA Vice-President and member of FIFA Executive Committee during the meeting held in Vienna in 1994.

54. The early 2000s of TFF under the management of Haluk Ulusoy could be named as Turkish football's golden years. The investments made in footballing infrastructure, training and facilities started to pay off, and the achievements of the National Team and clubs started to become a classic.

55. The most remarkable international success of Turkish football at club level was achieved in 2000. Galatasaray, which held the title at the end of the 1998–1999 seasons, qualified for the Champions League on 11 August 1999.

56. On 17 May 2000, Fatih Terim's squad won the UEFA Cup when the final whistle was blown in the game, which, including the extra time, ended with no scoring. However, Galatasaray defeated Arsenal on penalties 4-1 and won the UEFA Cup.

57. In between these two historic successes achieved by Galatasaray, the National Team played in the 2000 European Championship quarter-final.

58. Turkish football enjoyed its most remarkable days in the summer of 2002. The National Team took the third place in FIFA World Cup 2002. Also, the National Team was granted the Fair Play Award for demonstrating fair play to the last by saluting the South Korean fans hand in hand with South Korean players, who were crying for losing the match at their home, Deagu.

59. Turkey failed to qualify for the UEFA 2004 European Championship finals and FIFA 2006 World Cup finals.

60. The incidents that took place after the FIFA 2006 World Cup play-off game played between Turkey and Switzerland on 16 November 2005 at Sükrü Saracoglu Stadium led to a crisis. After the game, the players attacked each other. The next morning FIFA announced that a severe disciplinary case has been opened against TFF. The disciplinary procedures took long time, and FIFA Disciplinary Committee rendered its decision on 7 February 2006. TFF was found guilty of violation of Article 50, Article 70 let. b, c, d and e of the FIFA Disciplinary Code (FDC) and held liable in application of Article 70ff paragraph 1. TFF was ordered to pay a fine of CHF 200,000. In accordance with Articles 24 and 25 FDC, TFF was ordered to play its next six official home matches behind closed doors on a neutral ground in another country affiliated to UEFA, with a minimum distance of 500 km to the Turkish border.

61. Upon the decision of the FIFA Disciplinary Committee, TFF appealed to the FIFA Appeals Committee; however, with its decision on 7 April 2007, the Appeals Committee rejected TFF's appeal and decided to approve the decision of the FIFA Disciplinary Committee.

62. TFF requested a review of the decision from the FIFA Appeals Committee. For the first time in FIFA's history, the Committee accepted to review the case and decided on 24 June 2006. TFF was ordered to play its next three official home matches behind closed doors on a neutral ground in another country affiliated to UEFA with a minimum distance of 500 km to the Turkish border.

63. The National Team played its first three home games in Germany for the UEFA Euro 2008 European Football Championship. Despite all the complications of the said disciplinary decision, the National Team managed to qualify for the UEFA Euro 2008 Tournament. The team's success was beyond expectations and left the tournament at semi-finals by losing the game against Germany.

64. Unfortunately, no significant sporting success has been achieved since UEFA 2008 European Football Championship.

65. In the summer of 2011, a match-fixing scandal burst in Turkish football. The summary of the events are as follows: in the season 2010–2011, Trabzonspor was leading the league. Fenerbahçe came from behind and won sixteen out of seventeen games. Although the points were even between the two clubs, Fenerbahçe's head-to-head record was better, so Fenerbahçe won the champion title. In the morning of 3 July 2011, it came out that Turkish Police had been investigating nineteen games on suspicion. Presidents, Executive Committee members, players, coaches, officials, ninety-three persons were accused, and thirty-one of them were arrested. At the end of long trials, twenty-one persons were sentenced for imprisonment because of their match-fixing activities. The president of Fenerbahçe criticized the case as political. He blamed the Fethullah Gulen community; he pointed out that there was a shadowy network between the police, jurisdiction and Fethullah Gulen and that the investigation's only aim was to get over Fenerbahçe. After the recognition of Fethullah Gulen community as a terrorist group by the government, the then Prime Minister Recep Tayyip Erdoğan also declared his opinion over this match-fixing scandal as a well-designed, carefully calculated act of F.G. Terrorist Group. After a short while, all the defendants were acquitted, and the special authority courts were abolished by the Grand National Assembly. After the investigations held following the failed coup in July 2016, the police chief, public prosecutors and judges of the match-fixing investigation and jurisdiction turned out to be members of F.G. Terrorist Group.

66. Following 3 July 2011, TFF also involved in the prosecution phase and handed all the files over to its headquarters to begin disciplinary proceedings regarding the allegations. The Disciplinary and other related Regulations of TFF in force in 2011 were punishing any party involved in the match-fixing acts by relegation. Then TFF's President Mehmet Ali Aydınlar called the General Assembly of TFF with the agenda that the regulations be toned down. The General Assembly was held on 26 January 2012, and the members of the General Assembly did not accept this proposition. On 31 January 2012, President Mehmet Ali Aydınlar resigned and new elections were held. Yıldırım Demirören was elected as the new President of TFF on 27 February 2012. The Ethics Committee investigated the case, and its decision might be summarized as: although there have been some acts of match-fixing, the results of these acts did not affect the game played on the pitch. After this 'relaxing' decision of the Ethics Committee, the Executive Committee of TFF held a meeting. At this meeting, the Ex. Co. amended the regulations and toned down the punishments applicable to match-fixing acts. Moreover, it declared that disciplinary proceedings have been opened against all the Clubs, presidents, directors, managers, coaches, players and other officials who are involved in the match-fixing investigation of the police department. Professional Football Disciplinary Committee rendered its decision on 7 May 2012, announcing that only several officials were punished by one–three years of ban from footballing activities and none of the Clubs were found guilty. On 4 June 2012, the Appeals Committee confirmed the decisions of the Disciplinary Committee. Although several applications were made by Trabzonspor to declare them as the champion of the 2010–2011 season, all the applications have been rejected by TFF.

67. UEFA appointed a disciplinary inspector to investigate and submit a report to decide whether the case should be forwarded to UEFA Control and Disciplinary Body. After the report of the disciplinary inspector, proceedings opened against Fenerbahçe and Beşiktaş. UEFA Control and Disciplinary Body decided that both clubs were involved in match-fixing and banned Fenerbahçe for a total of two seasons for which they qualify for either the Champions League or Europa League, with the ban for the third campaign deferred for a probationary period of five years. Beşiktaş was banned for the next season's Europa League. Both clubs appealed the UEFA Control and Disciplinary Body's decision; the Appeals Committee decided to reject Beşiktaş's appeal, partially upheld the decision and lifted the probationary period.

In 2014, UEFA launched an investigation against Sivasspor and Eskişehirspor. Disciplinary Body declared that Eskişehirspor and Sivasspor were not eligible to participate in the 2014/2015 UEFA Europa League. Both Sivasspor and Eskişehirspor appealed to the Court of Arbitration for Sport (CAS); however, CAS upheld the decisions.

68. The match-fixing trials were still pending before both the national and international judicial bodies. After the special authority courts were abolished and relations between the chief of police, prosecutors and judges with the F.G. Terrorist Group revealed, all the accused and sentenced persons were acquitted. Fenerbahçe had asked the Supreme Court to confirm the decision of release. Trabzonspor made several complaints before UEFA against TFF and Fenerbahçe in order to be declared the champion of 2010–2011 season. However, UEFA rejected Trabzonspor's claims; CAS also confirmed the decisions. Lastly, Trabzonspor lodged a claim at FIFA; FIFA rejected the claim of Trabzonspor. Trabzonspor appealed to CAS in 2019. CAS confirmed FIFA's decision. Trabzonspor appealed to the Swiss Federal Court. Finally, the Swiss Federal Court rejected Trabzonspor's appeal in the year 2020.

69. This match-fixing scandal caused Turkish football an irreparable damage. Hatred between Trabzonspor and Fenerbahçe fans continues, the interest in football decreased dramatically, people lost their faith in fair play and true game. Despite nearly seven years past over the scandal, the increase in match-day revenues is still too low than expected.

70. In 2013, TFF hosted FIFA U-20 World Cup. The organization was successful, and nearly 300,000 fans attended the games.

B. Legal Nature

71. As we have briefly stated above, TFF has been established and gained its autonomy by a special law. By having a special law, TFF constitutes one of the rare examples throughout FIFA member associations.[2]

72. On 17 June 2002, the Turkish Parliament enacted Law No. 3813 named as: Law of Establishment and Objectives of TFF. Being a part of continental-law system, the law regulated the Federation and function, bodies, incomes, outcomes, etc., in detail.

73. The last amendment was done by the Turkish Parliament on 4 December 2007 with Law No. 5719. Before this amendment, Article 31[3] having the title of 'Supervision and Inspection of the Ministry' was a big question mark on FIFA's

2. Please *see* Annex I.
3. Supervision and Inspection of the Ministry of State: Art. 31 (amended on 20 Apr. 2000–4563/12). Primarily the national and international competitions and all the activities and operations of the Federation are subject to the supervision and inspection the State Minister responsible for sports.

mind. According to FIFA, this article was a direct intervention of the government, and this was unacceptable. FIFA warned TFF several times about this article and the whole structure of the law. Article 31 must be removed from the law immediately, and the law should be a framework law. Whole procedures and details should be regulated in the statute of TFF.

74. However, working on a new statute and a frame law could take more time than FIFA's deadline. On 4 December 2007, the Turkish Parliament made several amendments on Law No. 3813, including removal of Article 31. According to this amendment, the General Assembly of TFF called for an extraordinary meeting. At this extraordinary meeting, elections for presidency and board were held, and a study group was appointed. This study group worked with FIFA and prepared a new statute.

75. At the ordinary General Assembly meeting of TFF, which was held on 3 June 2008, the aforementioned new statute was accepted by the General Assembly unanimously.

76. On 5 May 2009, the new law of TFF was enacted by the Turkish Parliament, and it is Law No. 5894 on the Establishment and Duties of TFF. In the following paragraph, the new law will be explained. When the new law is compared with the old Law No. 3813, the main difference is the content of the law. The old one was more traditional and tried to fill every gap type of law; therefore, it had thirty-four articles. The new law has a frame law characteristic; it solely put the main principles and let the statute fill the gaps.

77. The Law on the Establishment and Duties of TFF contains twenty-one articles. Titled 'Objective', the first article sets the main purpose and legal structure of the Federation as:

> The objective of this Law is to set out the principles and procedures regarding the establishment, organizational structure, duties and powers of the Turkish Football Federation, a self-governing association subject to private law, to conduct, organize and develop all kinds of football activities in accordance with the related national and international laws and also to represent Turkey in Turkey and abroad on subjects related to football.

78. With the first article, it has clearly been set out that the Federation is 'autonomous/self-governing' and 'subject to private law'.

Following the investigation to be held by the High Inspection Committee of the Prime Minister, the State Minister responsible for Sports may summon the General Assembly for the extraordinary meeting to decide whether the President of the Federation and the Executive Committee has to be suspended or not, if their respective activities are deemed to create a drawback by staying in the office.

79. Being subject to private law is also a condition to have autonomous structure. In the past years, a lot of TFF executive board's decisions over football have been challenged before Administrative Courts. Thanks to Article 1 that all the courts rejected the claims because of lack of jurisdiction. Said decisions have also been approved by the Counsel of State.

80. TFF's legal status is sui generis. Being autonomous and subject to private law clearly distinguishes TFF from governmental organizations; thus, TFF cannot be classified as a 'federation' by means of the Law of Associations.

81. In Law No. 5253 Law of Associations, federation has been defined as a union which has been formed by associations. In Law No. 5894, 'membership' has been regulated. Despite the fact that the member associations are FCs and other associations are having a role in football family, the formation of TFF is distinct from the traditional definition of 'federation'.

82. When the decisions of the General Assembly were brought to the Courts of Law, the courts decided on the case by evaluating Law No. 5894 and the Civil Code and Law of Associations by analogy.

C. Bodies and Functions

83. Article 4 having the title 'Organization' of Law No. 5894 states that:

1. The organization of the TFF shall be set out in the TFF Statutes.
2. The organization of the TFF shall be composed of its Head-office and both affiliated domestic and overseas offices. The Head-office of the TFF is in Ankara.
3. All football organizations in Turkey shall be legally subordinated to the TFF and their respective rights and responsibilities shall be described by the TFF Statutes and regulations.
4. TFF is a member of both FIFA and UEFA.
5. The central organization of the TFF shall consist of at least the following organs:
   a. Congress.
   b. President.
   c. Executive Board.
   d. Emergency Committee.
   e. Legal Committees.
   f. Audit Committee.
   g. General Secretary.
6. The consultative and administrative units of TFF shall consist of the following bodies:
   a. General Secretariat.
   b. Standing and Ad-Hoc Committees.

7. The members of the TFF organs and committees shall either be appointed or elected in accordance with the TFF Statute.
8. Elections for all TFF organs shall be held by means of free and independent democratic procedures.

1. Congress

84. The Congress has only been named in the law and the principles are set out in the Statute. The Congress holds meeting every year until 31 July; electoral Congress holds its ordinary meeting once every four years, within forty-five days from the registration date of the Turkish football leagues at a date which is decided by the Executive Committee.

85. At the yearly Congress meetings, the activity programme and budget of TFF are approved, and the Executive Committee is authorized to make modifications to the budget when necessary, and the Executive Committee and the President are acquitted.

86. The Congress' objectives are listed under Article 23 of the statute. The most important objectives can be summarized as: to elect the president and the executive board members, to establish and amend statute, to authorize the Executive Committee for the purchase and sale of property, to approve the audit report issued by the Auditing Committee every year, etc.

87. The members of the Congress are listed under Article 22 of the statute. All the clubs that compete at the Super League, First League, Second League and Third League have the right to be represented at the Congress. However, the representation is not equal; for example, a Super League Club is represented by seven delegates, a First League Club is represented by two delegates and Second League and Third League Clubs are represented only by their presidents. Also, delegates from the Amateur Sports Clubs Federation, past TFF presidents, Professional Footballers' Association, presidents of the disabled federations, etc., are represented at the Congress. In every Congress, the number of the member varies; however, the estimated list of members is around 290 – 43% of the members are the representatives of the Super League Clubs, 12% of the members are the representatives of the First League Clubs, 12% of the members are the representatives of the Second League, 18% of the members are the representatives of the Third League Clubs, and the remaining 15% of the members are the representatives of the other football stakeholders.

88. The clubs hold the majority with 85%. The football players are represented by 2%, the technical directors are represented by 2%, amateur football is represented by 3% and the referees are represented by 3%. These numbers help us to understand how fairly the other stakeholders of football are represented at the Congress of their Federation.

2. Presidency

89. The term of office for the President is four years. The election of the President is held before the election of the fourteen members of the Executive Committee at the Congress.

90. The most important objectives of the President shall be listed as: to represent the Federation, to chair the executive committee, to propose to the Executive the formation and nominees for the subsidiary committees, the president, the principal and substitute members of the Referees' Committee and the president and members of the Appeals Committee and the president of the Dispute Resolution Chamber, etc.

3. Executive Committee

91. The Executive Committee is composed of fifteen members, including the President of the Federation and fourteen members elected by the Congress.

92. The Congress elects an equal number of substitute members. The term of the Executive Committee is four years.

93. The most important objectives of the executive committee shall be listed as: to register the FCs; to classify them into divisions and groups; to determine the names of the leagues; to organize the leagues; to determine the conditions of the promotion and relegation; to ratify the result of the matches; to postpone the matches; to adjust the dates; to decide on the matches which are unfinished, fixed and with incidents; to arrange and audit all commercial and financial rights for television, radio; to decide on the applications of clubs, football players, technical managers and coaches, referees, match officials and other personnel working related to football who are not in the jurisdiction of Dispute Resolution Chamber and Disciplinary Committees; to prepare the budget; to appoint the president, the principal and substitute members of the Referee's Committee and the president and members of the Appeals Committee and the President of the Dispute Resolution Chamber proposed by the President, etc.

94. Also, an Emergency Committee is defined under the statute to deal with all matters requiring immediate settlement between two Executive Committee meetings. The Emergency Committee shall consist of the President of TFF, the vice-presidents and two Executive Committee members to be appointed by the President. The term of office of the Emergency Committee shall be limited to that of the Executive Committee. Decisions passed by the Emergency Committee meetings shall take effect immediately and be approved by the Executive Committee in its next meeting.

4. Auditing Committee

95. Auditing Committee is composed of five members and five substitute members who have expertise in financial matters and are elected by the General Assembly for the term of four years.

96. The Auditing Committee audits the financial activities of the Federation prepared by the Executive Committee and accepted by the Congress according to the regulation, on behalf of the Congress.

5. Appeals Committee

97. The Appeals Committee will be explained in detail in Part 1 Chapter 1 *infra.*

6. Referees' Committee

98. The Referees' Committee is composed of nine members and nine substitute members, including a President, among those who are inactive referees at least for one year, nominated upon the proposal of the President of Federation and by approval of the Executive Committee. Also, those who did not perform as referee but have experience in sports shall be nominated to serve in the Referee's Committee; however, the number of these nominees shall not exceed three.

99. The Referees' Committee manages the official and friendly matches between FCs, resolves technical disputes related to the laws of the game, establishes the Provincial and County Referees' Committees, educates and classifies the referees, sets out the conditions for promotion and relegation and performs other duties set forth in the statutes and regulations.

100. Moreover, the Referees' Committee performs its functions independently. Unless a member resigns or is deemed to have been resigned, he may not be replaced.

7. Dispute Resolution Chamber

101. The Dispute Resolution Chamber will be explained in detail in Part 1 Chapter 1 *infra.*

8. Disciplinary Committees

102. Disciplinary Committees are composed of Provincial Disciplinary Committees, Amateur Football Disciplinary Committee and Professional Football Disciplinary Committee.

103. Amateur Football Disciplinary Committee and Professional Football Disciplinary Committee are appointed by the proposal of the President and approval of the Executive Committee. Provincial Disciplinary Committees are appointed by the proposal of the Amateur Affairs Committee and approval of the President. Both Amateur and Professional Football Committees are composed of one President and six members. Provincial Disciplinary Committees are composed of one President, and in accordance with the sporting activities of the province, the number of members shall be at least two up to a maximum of four members. Substitute members are appointed to the Committees. Disciplinary Committees are in office as long as the President's office.

104. All the members shall hold a two-year or four-year university degree. President, vice-president and secretary shall be graduates of a Law School.

105. Both the Professional and Amateur Disciplinary Committees have meetings two times a week. In case of emergency, they also decide to have a meeting other than these two meetings.

9. Standing Committees

106. The President and the members of the Standing Committees necessary to perform the activities and transactions of the Federation are appointed by the President of the Federation with the approval of the Executive Committee. The Executive Committee may, if necessary, create ad hoc committees for special duties and for a limited period of time. The Executive Committee appoints its members and approves its terms of references.

107. Standing Committees are as follows:

(a) Referee's Committee.
(b) Committee of Delegates.
(c) Sports Medical Committee.
(d) International Relations Committee.
(e) Committee of Social Responsibility and Fair Play.
(f) Other Standing Committees.

10. General Secretariat

108. The General Secretary is the chief executive of the General Secretariat and is under the authority of the Executive Committee. The General Secretary shall be appointed by the Executive Committee upon the proposal of the President of TFF.

D. Regulations

109. With the power and duty given by law, TFF's Executive Committee has to set out all the necessary Regulations in order to operate TFF. Today, TFF has thirty-six Regulations in force. Names of the most important Regulations and a brief explanation about some of them are given below:

- Football Competition Regulation (August 2017).
- Regulations for the Status and Transfer of Professional Player (August 2016).
- Disciplinary Code (August 2017).
- Regulation Governing the Procedure of the Appeals Committee (August 2017).
- Regulation Governing the Procedure of the Dispute Resolution Chamber (June 2019).
- TFF Club Licensing and Financial Fair Play Regulations (June 2019).
- Stadium and Security Committee's Regulation (August 2006).
- Accreditation Regulation (August 2018).
- Regulation Governing the Expenditure of Fund (July 2009).
- Media Regulation (August 2019).
- Media Regulation for Super League and First League (August 2019).
- Kit Regulation (August 2016).
- Regulation Governing the Registration of FCs (June 2009).
- Amateur Player's License and Transfer Regulation (October 2008).
- Jubilee Regulation of Professional Players (June 2009).
- Regulation for the Technical Coaches' Statute and Working Conditions (August 2018).
  Regulation for the Technical Coaches' Education and Classification (August 2018).
- Referee's Committee Regulation (August 2020).
- Officers' Committee Regulation (August 2020).
- Provincial Representative and Organization Committees Regulation (August 2006).
- Fair Play Regulation (July 2019).
- Medical Crew Regulation (June 2009).
- Football for Everyone Regulation (February 2009).
- Regulation for Friendly Games and Tournaments (July 2015).
- Ethics Committee Regulation (December 2009).
- Regulation of Football Academies (April 2010).
- Regulation of Club Registration (June 2009).

1. Football Competition Regulation

110. This regulation's objective is to organize and set out all the basic rules regarding both professional and amateur competitions.

111. Titles of some of the articles are: the kinds of matches, principles of scoring and average system, principles of knock-out system, the results of an unfinished match, postponed matches; conditions of annulment of a match result, point deduction; objection procedures of a match, etc.

2. Regulations for the Status and Transfer of Professional Player

112. As a member of FIFA, TFF is obligated to harmonize its Regulation for the Status and Transfer of Professional Player in conformity with the FIFA's regulation.

113. Thanks to TFF's professionals, from the first FIFA's regulation until the last revision of 2010, TFF has always enacted its own regulation and created its own system which constitutes one of the best practices throughout Europe.

114. Below, you may find some of the important articles of the said regulation which also reflect the main structure of the transfer system of TFF.

a. Status of a Player

115. The regulation begins with a clear definition of the status of the player. A professional player is defined as:

> **Professional Player**
>
> A professional is a player who has a written contract with a club and is paid more for his footballing activity than the expenses he effectively incurs.

116. The above definition is a word-to-word translation of the said FIFA's Regulation Article 2.2.

117. However, an amateur player is defined more in detail:

> **Amateur Player**
>
> 1. The players who are other than the ones defined in Article 3 are accepted as amateur players.
> 2. The costs related with a match like accommodation, insurance, kit and training shall not affect the player's amateur status.
> 3. Amateur players shall not play in the professional league and cup tournaments.

118. On the contrary, in several European countries, amateur players do not have any written contract with their clubs. The amateurs are the ones who are accepted to be the new generation of professional football or the ones who are older and may be less talented players and play football for fun or health reasons. For the past few years, TFF has been paying more attention to amateur football and has been planning new projects in order to increase the number of amateur-licensed players.

b. Transfer of a Professional Player

119. Since it is obligatory to sign a contract between a player and a club, it can be stated that the transfer begins with the signing of a contract during one of the two transfer periods.

120. Article 14 having the title 'Application of Registration' states the procedure to be followed while signing a professional player's contract:

> Article 14 – Application of Registration
>
> (1) The registration process of professional players to clubs is carried out digitally via FYS (Football Administration System).
> (2) In case it is determined that the documents submitted by the clubs in the digital registration application are not correct and in accordance with the original, the provisions of the Football Competition Regulation and the Disciplinary Code shall be applied.
> (3) Clubs are obliged to authorise a person with e-signature to use the digital licence system.
> (4) For the digital licence process, the following documents must be uploaded to the FYS system, without prejudice to the provisions of Article 12 of this Regulation, provided that the originals are kept by the club in accordance with the legal legislation:
>   a) Contract signed by the parties (If the contract is presented in a foreign language, a notary sworn Turkish translation)
>   b) Notarised signature circular showing the persons authorised to represent the club,
>   c) Receipt of the amount to be deposited to the TFF Social Assistance and Solidarity Foundation account during the registration and visa procedures determined by the TFF every year,
>   d) Photograph of the player (It must be dated 6 months before the transaction date at the latest.)
>   e) Other documents to be requested by TFF according to licence types.

In case any of the documents mentioned above are not submitted, contracts shall not be registered and licences shall not be issued. In the event that the club has a transfer ban within the scope of Article 12 of this Regulation, if other documents are available, only the professional player contracts that the club will sign with its own players whose contracts have expired or are ongoing and amateur players who have been registered with it for the last six months will be registered, other contracts will not be registered, and licences will not be issued.

121. Loan of professionals is enacted under Article 15; however, 'provisional transfer' term is being used instead of 'loan of professionals' in the regulation. Therefore, both 'provisional transfer' and 'loan of professionals' terms will be used in the monograph:

Article 14 – Provisional Transfer

1. A professional may be loaned to another club on the basis of a written agreement between him and the clubs concerned.
2. The minimum loan period shall be the time between two registration periods.
3. If the player returns to his original club at the end of the loan period, then the registration for the provisional transfer and the registration for the original club shall be accepted as one registration.
4. When the provisional transfer contract ends, the player is registered under his original club only in the transfer period.
5. The conditions restricting the sportive competition and the matches which is the player will participate of the provisional transfer contract is unacceptable.

122. Unfortunately, TFF still could not adopt new FIFA RSTP articles relating to loan of professional players.

c. Training Compensation

123. The training compensation system is nearly being adopted as the same as the one in FIFA's Regulation with a few differences.

124. The categories and the amounts are decided by the Executive Committee at the beginning of each season. For 2023–2024 season, the categories and their amount have been declared at the Executive Committee's meeting for the national transfers:

First Category	Super League Clubs	TRL 500,000
Second Category	1st League Clubs	TRL 250,000
Third Category	2nd League Clubs	TRL 100,000
Fourth Category	3rd League Clubs and Amateur Clubs	TRL 50,000

125. The most important difference from FIFA's system is that: it is compulsory for the new and old clubs to agree on training compensation and submit the document thereof to TFF at the application of registration phase. The thirty-day period in FIFA's Regulation is not given to the new Club in TFF's Regulation.

126. According to TFF's system, the education and training of a player begins from his/her age of 12 years to 23 years. In principle, the compensation is payable at each transfer of the player until his/her age of 23 years.

127. Furthermore, there are some precautions that have been enacted in order to prevent clubs from cheating the system by transferring a player to a lower category and then transferring him/her back the following season and/or signing a loan agreement in order to avoid paying the training compensation.

128. Since the training compensation is obligatory and has been implemented without any concession, the clubs generally agree upon an amount or do protocols on receiving certain percentage of players' further transfers.

129. From the first day of this regulation until now, none of the parties has challenged the training system before the Executive Committee or Appeals Committee. Today, it is still a question mark what would the Dispute Resolution Chamber's decision be if a club challenges that a player has completed his/her training period before the age of 23 years.

d. Duties of the Parties

130. Article 24, having the title 'Obligation of Clubs', of the said Regulation states that:

> Any club which signed contracts with professional players shall fulfil its obligations other than the contracts are:
>
> a. Safeguard its players' health and take all measures necessary for matches, training activities, camps and travels in accordance with the provisions regarding health and injuries;
> b. To maintain all the necessary sporting kit for the players;
> c. Clubs are obliged to send their internal regulations and/or disciplinary regulations to be implemented in the following season to the TFF at the latest one week before the start of the season. Clubs are obliged to deliver the internal regulations and/or disciplinary regulations that they have registered with the TFF and that they will implement to the player against signature or to notify them through a notary public;
> d. In cases where it imposes a fine on any of its players, provide such player and the Federation with a notarized copy of its decision. While doing so, the information about the amount of fine and the reason shall be given and this notification shall be sent within 15 days of such decision of the Executive Committee of the Club;
> e. If the Club's Executive Committee decides to exclude a player from the squad, then the club has to prepare a training program, appoint at least a coach and a training facility for the excluded player;
> f. Take out insurance from its professional players from private insurers, which are determined by the Federation, against risks of permanent and

partial injury, accident and death that may be incurred during matches, training activities to be performed, whether in Turkey or abroad, and during travels to and from the venues of such matches.

g. Prepare and submit necessary documents for the player's military service with the player himself.
h. Clubs shall have all their players who will play in professional league and cup competitions undergo a medical examination at a fully-fledged hospital and obtain a medical board report stating that they do not have any disability to play football; keep the relevant documents in accordance with the legal regulations and submit them to the TFF upon request;

131. Some of the obligations of the clubs are quite rare in European Regulations. Below, you may find a brief explanation about the most important sub-articles.

132. Unfortunately, it is very common in Turkish clubs to impose fine on players without any justified reason. In the past years, it has been seen that players even did not have any knowledge about this fine or the reason thereof. The first aim of the article is to make sure that the player and TFF are aware of the fine. The second is to prevent the bad faith by setting a deadline. The document is again requested as notarized in order to fix the date and prevent those who may cheat on previous Executive Committee documents.

133. The clubs commonly impose fine with a purpose of deducting the fine from the players' fee. When a player challenges the decision of the club before the Dispute Resolution Chamber, this bad faith of clubs is evaluated by the Chamber and said kind of fines are fully annulled.

134. From the previous versions of the Regulation until today, the sub-article (c) and (d) helped football players to reduce the abuse thereof.

135. Sub-article (e) is also another problem for players. When a player is not content with his/her club, he/she may constitute a problem for the whole team. After the failure of several attempts to win him/her back for the team, then the only stand is to exclude him/her. However, this sanction or precaution could damage the players' professional lives seriously, and no one has the right to end someone's career in this way. Therefore, TFF by forcing clubs to appoint a coach and a training facility for the excluded player tried to reduce the possible damages for the player's professional life.

136. Sub-article (f) came out because of such grievous experiences. Before this system was recognized, the players had no insurance for accidents, injuries, etc. More than fifteen years ago, this system worked perfectly; however, in the past few years, the Clubs began to complain about the high premium amounts. As a first step, TFF centralized the system and opened a bid for more than thousand professional players' insurance premiums. This bidding process really lowered the premium, and the clubs were satisfied with the result. From season 2006–2007, by a decision of the then Executive Committee, TFF began to pay for all the premiums and the following Executive Committees did not disturb this tradition.

137. Article 25, having the title 'Obligations of the Players', of the said Regulation states that:

> Any player who signed a contract with a Club shall fulfil his obligations other than the contracts are:
>
> a. To follow up, complete and ensure the necessary documents and other transactions in order to participate in the matches,
> b. To participate courses, lessons or seminars prepared by the Club or TFF,
> c. In the case of illness or injury, transmit his health and injury reports to his club and the Federation within ten days (any player failing to do so shall not be entitled to claim any rights arising from such illness or injury),

138. The players have fewer obligations than the clubs. The subparagraphs of (c) and (d) are the most important ones.

139. Subparagraph (c) came after a serious number of abuses. In order to get a new and a better contract, football players invented kinds of methods like leaving one club without any notice to the other club's test training and return home when the new club does not wish to sign a contract with him/her. The first thing that comes to their mind is to lie about their absence, and the most common lie is to state that they were ill. Unfortunately, they have a 'good' relationship with the medicals that they can obtain a health report. In order to avoid this kind of abuse, TFF gives a ten-day period to the player to notify the club and the Federation.

e. Termination

140. If a party of a contract fails to fulfil his/her liabilities, as making a payment to the other party, the Code of Obligations gives a clear right to the party to terminate the contract immediately:

> b) Immediate Termination Article 107 – There is no need for giving an extension period under below listed circumstances.
>
> …
>
> 3. If the debt should have been paid at a certain period of time as it is stated in the contract.

141. As an exception of the Code of Obligations, termination of a professional player's contract can only be registered if the said termination has been done in conformity with the procedure that has been set out by the Regulation.

142. To set a procedure for the termination was inevitable; an unstable league would be unacceptable. If TFF had not set a procedure for the termination, the clubs would have never known their squad for the next game. The relevant articles of the regulation are as follows:

> VI. Termination of the Contract and Consequences Thereof
>
> Article 26 – Termination by Mutual Consent
> In order to register the termination of the contract by mutual consent the documents given below shall be submitted to TFF:
>
> (1) In order for the mutual termination to be recorded in the records, it is obligatory to digitally submit the relevant agreement to the TFF via FYS together with a copy of the notarised signature circular identifying the persons authorised to represent the club.
> (2) It is obligatory to keep the originals of the aforementioned documents at the club.
> (3) In case it is determined that the documents submitted by the clubs are not true and correct, the provisions of the Football Competition Regulation and the Disciplinary Code shall be applied.
>
> Article 27 – Club's Right of Termination
>
> 1. Below listed circumstances constitute just cause for the termination:
>   a. Any kind of illness or injury of the player which exceeds six months.
>   b. If the player is banned for at least six months by the Disciplinary Committees.
>   c. Serious breach of Article 25 by the player.
>   d. If the Player has been punished with a ban at least for 4 games for his violation of Regulations on Working with Intermediaries.
>
>   Except subparagraph c stated below, any Club who will exercise its right of immediate termination then it shall exercise this right within thirty days of player's violation and should send a letter from notary public for termination. Any termination, done after the thirty-day time limit expires, shall not be deemed as just cause.
> 2. If the player is in default of his contractual liabilities to the Club or violates subparagraph c of this article, and if the Club is willing to terminate the contract, then the club should send a notarized warning letter to the player and give him at least seven day time to act in appropriate with the contract. Despite receiving the notarized letter If the player does not fulfil his obligations then the Club has right to terminate the contract in seven days following the end of given time period.
>
> Article 28 – Player's Right of Termination
>
> 1. If the Club is in default of paying fee, and if the player is willing to terminate the contract, then the player should send a notarized warning to the club and give them thirty days of time to pay his dues. Despite receiving

the notarized letter if the club does not fulfil his obligations then the player has the right to terminate the contract in seven days following the end of given time period.

2. If the Club is in default of its other contractual liabilities, and if the player is willing to terminate the contract, then the player should send a notarized warning to the club and give at least thirty days of time to act in appropriate with the contract. Despite receiving the notarized letter if the club does not fulfil his obligations then the player has the right to terminate the contract in seven days following the end of given time period.
3. Above-mentioned time limits shall not be changed to the detriment of the player.
4. After receiving the notification set out in paragraph (1), TFF, shall notify the Club at latest in seven days via facsimile or any type of communication. The time limits set out in the paragraph (1) shall begin from whichever comes first either TFF's notification or Notary Public's notification. Moreover, TFF shall send the document evidencing the notification date to the player or his attorney.
5. Any player older than 23 years of age who has, in the course of the season, appeared in fewer than 10% of the official matches in which his club has been involved may terminate his contract prematurely on the ground of sporting just cause. Due consideration shall be given to the player's circumstances in the appraisal of such cases.
6. A player may only terminate his contract on this basis in the fifteen days following the last official match of the club with which he is registered.

Article 29 – Procedure of Termination

1. Terminating party shall declare his will with a notarized letter of notice and shall send one copy of the letter to TFF.
2. When the TFF receives the termination letter, registers it and notify this transaction to the parties.
3. In case of a termination, a player shall only transfer to a new club, if the new club accepts to be liable severally with the player in written.

143. It is quite evident that the regulation has no equilibrium between the club and the player. The previous versions of the regulation were more protective of the player. It is quite naive to expect a player to notify and give thirty days of time to the club and maintain his sporting career in peace. The clubs may fall into a habit of not paying the fees until receiving a notification letter from the player and/or paying it on the twenty-ninth day.

144. After the thirty-day period ends, the player has the right to terminate the contract within seven days. Seven days is quite a short time in the course of a season – think of a player who has to join a two-day camp programme before an away match, plus one day for the trip, the next day is the match day, the following day returning back home, and he/she suddenly finds that it is the sixth day, he/she has to control the bank account after that only he/she can go to the notary public and send the club a letter of termination (could help us to understand the situation in which the player might be).

145. Through termination, the balance between the parties of the contract shall be set in this new version of the regulation.

146. The consequences of terminating a contract without just cause are given below:

Article 30 – Sporting Sanctions

1. In addition to the obligation to pay compensation, sporting sanctions shall also be imposed on any player or club (except Article 27/1 a, b and d) who found to be terminating the contract without just cause during the protected period.
2. If a player is terminating his contract without just cause in the above-mentioned protected period, a sporting sanction of four months shall be imposed on him. In the case of aggravating circumstances, sporting sanction shall last six months. This sporting sanction shall be notified to the player and related Clubs. The execution of the sanction shall begin from the first official match which will be played after the mid-season break, if the sanction has been given after the expiry of the football season then the execution shall begin from the following new season's first official match.
3. Unilateral breach without just cause or sporting just cause after the protected period shall not result in sporting sanctions. Disciplinary measures may, however, be imposed outside the protected period for failure to give notice of termination within fifteen days of the last official match of the season of the club with which the player is registered.
4. The protected period starts again when, the contract is renewed or the duration of the previous contract is extended.
5. In addition to the obligation to pay compensation, sporting sanctions shall be imposed on any club found to be in breach of contract or found to be inducing a breach of contract during the protected period. It shall be presumed, unless established to the contrary, that any club signing a professional who has terminated his contract without just cause has induced that professional to commit a breach. The club shall be banned from registering any new players, either nationally or internationally, for two registration periods.
6. Any person (club officials, intermediaries, players, etc.) who acts in a manner designed to induce a breach of contract between a professional and a club in order to facilitate the transfer of the player shall be sanctioned.
7. Sporting sanctions shall be imposed by the Dispute Resolution Chamber if requested. Therefore, sporting sanctions shall be requested until the end of transfer period which is followed by the receipt of the notification of TFF mentioned in Art. 29. This period is a strict time limit.

147. By foreseeing heavy sporting sanctions, terminating contracts without just cause, or inducement of the player, has been possibly prevented. However, adopting international transfer rules to the national league might cause problems. In Article 30(5), the new club of the player is presumed to be the inducing party; however, it is predictable that national transfers are higher than international transfers in number. It is normal for a professional player to sign a new contract with a new club in the national league. For national transfers, the burden of proof should have been diverted to the sporting sanction requesting party. Today, the applicability of Article 30(5) is doubtful; if the Dispute Resolution Chamber strictly interprets the rule, most of the clubs would not be able to transfer new players for the following two transfer periods.

148. In order to secure parties' rights, Article 22bis was recently added to the Regulation as a reflection of Article 12 of FIFA Regulations on the Status and Transfer of Players (RSTP).

149. Another important article is 12th Article, which enables the creditor party put ban on transferring new players (for clubs) and playing (for players) until the debts are fully covered. This article does not apply automatically; the creditor should apply to TFF.

3. Regulation for the Technical Coaches' Statute and Working Conditions

150. The definition of the Technical Coach is given under the second Article of the Regulation as:

> Definitions: …
>
> g) COACH: Professional and amateur coaches,
> ğ) HEAD COACH: The coach who is responsible for team selection, tactics and training of the team before, during and at the end of the match, and for the management of the players and the technical team in the dressing room and technical area in accordance with the contract signed with the clubs.

151. The statute of a coach shall be either professional or amateur.

152. According to Article 5 of the said Regulation, foreign coaches shall only be permitted to work in the Super League, First League and Women's Teams.

153. Parties shall sign TFF's uniform contract, and the last day of the contract shall be 30 June. Moreover, according to Article 11, the remuneration shall not be under the minimum wage which is being declared by the government. A coach shall only work with a maximum of two clubs during one season.

154. Under Articles 12 and 13, the rights and duties of the parties have been listed. The duties of the club can be summarized as to maintain all the necessary conditions for the coach to be successful, give permission to the coach to participate in the seminars of TFF, inform the coach about the disciplinary sanctions that have been given by the club in fifteen days, etc. The duties of the coach can be summarized as to provide the best service for the club, not to bring the club into disrepute, in case of injury or illness to inform the club about it in five days after receiving the doctor's report, not to get advantage from a player's transfer, etc.

155. The conditions of bilateral termination of the contract between the club and the coach are subject to the same procedures as the players.

156. Club's right of termination has been regulated under Article 18 of the said Regulation as:

> Article 18 – Club's Right to Terminate the Contract
>
> (1) Below listed conditions constitute just cause for termination;
>   a) If coach's health problems regardless of the footballing activity exceeds the time period defined under Labour Code weeks,
>   b) To be sanctioned three or more months of ban from footballing activity by the Disciplinary Committees,
>   c) Not to contact with the Club consecutive three days or ten days or more in a season,
>   d) If the Coach has been punished with a ban from entering into dressing rooms and bench at least for 4 games for his violation of Regulations on Working with Intermediaries or this Regulation's Article 15.e.
>
> (2) If the coach fails to fulfil his duties, the Club shall notify the coach and shall give him a period of time to fulfil his duties. If the coach insists on not fulfilling his duties then the Club has the right to terminate the contract within seven days which is beginning at the end of the given period in the notification. The conditions of the first paragraph of this article are reserved.

157. Coach's right of termination has been regulated under Article 19 of the said Regulation as:

> Article 19 – Coach's Right to Terminate the Contract
>
> In case the Club fails to pay or fails fulfil his duties, if the coach's wish is to terminate the contract, then he should notify the Club and give it a period of time to fulfil its duties. If the Club insists on not fulfilling its duties then the coach has the right to terminate the contract within seven days which is beginning at the end of the given period in the notification.

In case of a dispute, parties are free to choose TFF's Dispute Resolution Chamber's jurisdiction. The decisions of the Dispute Resolution Chamber shall be appealed to the Appeals Committee.

4. Football Agent Regulations

158. When the new Law No. 7405 was being voted at the Grand National Assembly, by surprise an article regarding football agents was brought as proposal with enough signature of the Parliaments. This proposal was accepted by the Grand National Assembly, and 'Additional Article 2' was added to TFF's Law No. 5894 in the year 2022.

159. Agents Additional Article 2 – (Added: 7405 – 22.4.2022/ Article 54):

(1) Players, sports clubs and sports join-stock companies may benefit from the services of football agents in order to execute professional player contracts or transfer negotiations.
(2) The representation contract to be signed with the player must be made in the form of a notary public. The representation contract may be concluded for a maximum of two years. For minors who do not have the capacity to act, the signature of the guardian or custodian must be present.
(3) The representation contract must contain the names of the parties, the date and duration of the contract, the scope of the agent activity and the fee arising therefrom, payment terms, the agent's obligations, termination provisions and the signatures of the parties. In case the agent activity is carried out by a company, the company information must be included in the contract, and the trade registry certificate showing that the agent is authorized to represent the company must be attached to the contract.
(4) The signed representation contracts must be sent by the notary public to the Ministry of Youth and Sports and TFF within thirty days.
(5) In transfers, the amount of fee to be paid to the agent by the sports clubs and sports joint-stock companies and the payment conditions must be included in the contract to be signed between the sports clubs and sports joint-stock companies and the player. The fee of the agent acting on behalf of the player shall be calculated over the player's annual base gross income. In the calculation of the said gross income, other benefits such as gratuitous use of movable or immovable property or transfer of ownership, success bonuses or non-guaranteed benefits such as bonuses or privileges are not taken into account. The fee to be paid to the agent may be agreed up to 10% of this fee if the gross income to be paid to the player during the contract period is less than TRL 2 million, and up to 5% of this fee if the gross income is more than TRL 2 million.
(6) The agent representing the sports club or sports joint-stock company that transfers its football player to another club may agree to up to 10% of the endorsement fee obtained by the sports club or sports joint-stock company.
(7) The agent representing the sports club or sports joint-stock company that transfers its player to another club may be paid a fee up to 10% of the transfer fee obtained by the sports club or sports joint-stock company.

(8) A copy of the contract signed between the player and the sports clubs or sports joint-stock companies must be sent by the sports clubs and sports joint-stock companies to the Ministry of Youth and Sports and TFF within one week following the signing of the contract.
(9) In the event that any other legal transaction is detected between sports clubs, sports joint-stock companies and professional players and agents that provide direct or indirect benefits to the parties or third parties other than the contract notified to the Ministry of Youth and Sports and TFF, the agent's activity is terminated and the relevant player is banned from competitions from three months to one year. The president, board members and executives of the sports club and sports joint-stock company who act contrary to this paragraph shall be sentenced to deprivation of rights from two years to three years.
(10) The president, board members and executives of the sports club and sports joint-stock company shall be sentenced to imprisonment from one year to three years if they fail to comply with the fee limitations specified in the article.
(11) In case of failure to comply with the fee limitations specified in the article, the agent's licence shall be cancelled.
(12) If the contract notification obligation under this article is not complied with, the sanctions determined in the TFF regulations shall be imposed on the sports club and sports joint-stock company that do not comply with the notification obligation.
(13) Execution of agent service, qualifications that agents must have, ethical principles that agents must comply with while carrying out their duties, guiding principles to be followed by agents, training, qualifications of institutions and organizations that will provide training and permitting them, supervision and performance of agents, admission to, the procedures and principles regarding the joint-stock companies that will provide agent services and the qualifications to be carried by the persons who will work as agents within these companies, the annual activity reports to be prepared by agents and joint-stock companies, the procedures and principles regarding the keeping of the agent registry and other issues related to agent shall be determined by the TFF.

160. Following FIFA's new system, the new Regulation of TFF has been adopted and entered into force in November 2023.

161. The new regulation was almost in compliance with the FIFA Regulations; however, it was in contradiction with the Additional Article 2 in means of remuneration cap. There were also other problems; therefore, several clubs applied to TFF Appeals Committee. TFF Appeals Committee cancelled some of the articles of the TFF Regulation at its meeting held on 8 January 2024. Meanwhile, FIFA, with its circular letter of 1873, temporarily suspended the application of several articles of the Football Agent Regulations on 30 December 2023. Following this announcement and TFF Appeals Committee's decision, on 12 January 2024, TFF announced that the Football Agents Regulations have been repealed.

162. Until today, no roadmap has been determined and announced by the TFF regarding the uncertainty that has arisen.

5. Disciplinary Code

163. In August 2017, the Disciplinary Code was renewed. The Disciplinary Code is one of the most frequently changing regulations of TFF. TFF does not refrain from changing the Code during the course of a season.

164. The applicable sanctions which are defined in the Code are warning, reprimand, fine, return of awards, caution, expulsion, match suspension, ban from dressing rooms and substitutes' bench, stadium ban, ban on taking part in any footballing activity, transfer ban, playing a match on neutral ground, playing a match without spectators, ban on playing in a particular stadium, annulment of the results of a match, expulsion, relegation to a lower division, deduction of points, forfeit of a licence, suspension of a licence.

165. The infringements are defined in the Code as follows: misconduct, team misconduct, insult, violence, behaviours against TFF Regulations, media release or statements having unsporting character, media release or statements regarding referees, safety of referee's room and corridors, threats, coercion, forgery, failure to respect decisions, not to attend national matches, bad and unsavoury cheering, disrupting broadcast, manipulation of a match result, betting, not attending matches, breach of duty and corruption and doping.

166. Disciplinary proceedings at the professional leagues begin with disciplinary inspectors. The reports of the match officials read carefully and if an infringement against the Disciplinary Code is detected, proceedings begin against the club or other real person. The disciplinary proceedings at the Academy Leagues and Amateur League are subject to the same procedure; however, the deciding body is the Amateur Disciplinary Committee.

167. The Professional Football Disciplinary Committee notifies and asks for the relevant parties' defence. A forty-eight-hour defence period is given to the accused party. After receiving the defence, the Disciplinary Committee decides on the case. The decision of the Committee shall be appealed to the Appeals Committee in seven days. Both the accused party and disciplinary inspectors have the right to appeal the Committee's decision.

6. Regulation for Friendly Games and Tournaments

168. This new Regulation's scope is to bring order to the friendly games and tournaments which are being organized frequently.

169. An UEFA or FIFA match agent or a club shall be the organizer of such an event. The event shall be scheduled at the holiday breaks of a season, which is being declared at the beginning of the football season by TFF.

170. Under Article 6, a player's eligibility has been regulated as:

Article 6 – Player's Eligibility

1. As a rule, players registered with their club may play in friendly games and tournaments. However, a maximum of 2 players registered in other clubs affiliated to the TFF may play provided that the written approval of the clubs where these players are registered is obtained.
2. 'Player Health Report' must be obtained for the players who will take part in the aforementioned games or tournaments.

171. Article 8 having the title 'Friendly Games' brings limitations as: a club shall play friendly games only at the times when official games are ended in a season or a break is given by TFF and shall only play with the clubs who are members of a FIFA association, etc.

172. Article 9 having the title 'Tournaments' brings limitations as: a club shall participate in tournaments when official games are ended in a season or a break is given by TFF, if a club which is registered under another association shall submit the written approval of its relevant association or confederation, etc.

7. Regulations of Club Registration

173. This regulation covers the principles of club registration to TFF and its liabilities towards TFF. According to Turkish legislation, a sports club shall be established either as an association or as an incorporated company. Most of the Clubs have been established as an association. A minority of them transferred their football rights into an incorporated company. Most of the incorporated companies are also established by the association so to avoid the Club to be sold to any third person. Only few clubs are owned by a real or legal person.

174. The regulation basically reflects the common understanding of Civil Code, e.g., can choose any name and the same name cannot be used in the same city.

175. There are some exceptions; e.g., a club shall not be moved to another city.

176. Transferring of football activities of an association to an incorporated company is important. TFF requires from the association to transfer all rights and duties as a whole to an incorporated company. By doing so, TFF prevents associations in debt just to transfer their assets to an incorporated company and free themselves from their debts.

177. Four big clubs of the Turkish Super League, Galatasaray A.Ş, Beşiktaş A.Ş, Fenerbahçe A.Ş and Trabzonspor A.Ş are also listed on the stock exchange market: Borsa Istanbul. These clubs are also subject to capital boards of Turkey legislation.

E. Dispute Resolution

1. Dispute Resolution Chamber

178. Dispute Resolution Chamber has been listed as one of the first-instance legal committees in Article 5 of Law No. 5894. The Law refers to TFF's Statute for the duties and liabilities of each first-instance legal committee.

179. TFF's Statue Article 55 defines the Chamber. There is a Chairman's Committee of one president, six lawyers and six substitutes who are appointed by the Executive Board of TFF.

180. Article 56 foresees the duties of the Chamber; this arbitral Chamber decides on the contractual disputes between clubs and clubs; clubs and players, technical directors, coaches, intermediaries, physiotherapists; intermediaries and players, technical directors and coaches. The decisions of the Chamber shall become final and binding if there would not be any appeal to TFF's Appeals Committee.

181. The Dispute Resolution Chamber has an exclusive jurisdiction over the disputes regarding training compensation and claims of sporting sanctions.

2. The Appeals Committee

182. According to Law No. 5894 Article 6, TFF Appeals Committee is the sole appeals body. It examines and renders the final decisions upon the appeals lodged by the related parties against the decisions of the Executive Committee, Disciplinary Committees and Dispute Resolution Chamber as the final deciding body.

183. The Appeals Committee is composed of one Chairman, six members and six substitute members who are proposed by the President of the Federation and appointed by the Executive Committee.

184. The Committee is independent while performing its duties. Unless the members resign or are deemed to be resigned, new members shall not be appointed.

185. Since the Appeals Committee is appointed by the Executive Committee, its 'independence' is doubtful, especially when it comes to the decision of the Executive Committee.

3. Court of Arbitration for Sport

186. The CAS is recognized under Article 64 of the TFF's Statute.

187. According to Article 64, CAS is defined as an appeals body for a final decision given by either FIFA's or UEFA's jurisdictional bodies. However, the disputes regarding the laws of the game, exemptions foreseen at FIFA and UEFA Statutes and decisions of TFF's Appeals Committee shall not be appealed before CAS.

188. In the same article, TFF is obliged to ensure its affiliated clubs, players, officials, match agents and players' agents to comply with the final decisions of FIFA, UEFA or CAS.

189. According to Article 13 of TFF's Statute having the title 'Responsibilities of the Members' recognition of CAS is mandatory.

§3. The Turkish National Olympic Committee

190. The first establishment of the Turkish National Olympic Committee (TUMOK) falls in the period of the Ottoman era, in the nineteenth century. After the declaration of the Republic, Mr Selim Sırrı was appointed as the president of TUMOK. Finally, in 1962, TUMOK managed to fulfil the criteria of International Olympic Committee (IOC) and became an independent organization.

I. Legal Nature

191. TUMOK is an association established in accordance with the Civil Code.

192. Since TUMOK is subject to private law, the association has some special authorities which are given by the decision of the Cabinet. For example, the authority to cooperate with international organizations was given on 2 May 1970 Decision No. 7/191; hence, the authority to use the word 'Turkish' was also given by the decision of Cabinet. And on 16 July 1970 with the Decision No. 7/1070, the association was classified as 'working for the furtherance of public welfare' and gained some privileges, for example, having Value Added Tax (VAT) exemptions.

II. Bodies and Functions

193. In its statute, under Article 10, the bodies are listed as General Assembly, Executive Committee, Auditing Committee, Council, Registration Committee, High Counsel and Disciplinary Committee.

194. The General Assembly meets once in every two years with the participation of the members who have paid their annual fee. The duties of the General

Assembly can be summarized as electing the bodies of TUMOK, giving authority to the executive committee about legal transactions regarding the immovable property of the association, approving the audit report and yearly balance, etc.

195. The Executive Committee is elected by the General Assembly for a four-year period of time. All the members who have been a member for at least two years in the association could be a candidate for the executive committee. The General Assembly elects fifteen members and nine substitute members for the executive committee. The President is elected by the executive committee. The members of this committee are also the members of the Council.

196. Auditing Committee is composed of three members and three substitute members and they are elected by the General Assembly. The main duty of this committee is to audit the accounts of the association and prepare a report thereof.

197. The Council is composed of the members and substitute members of the Executive Committee, seven members and three substitute members that are elected by the General Assembly, one representative from each sports federation. The duties of the said Council are to determine the sports branches to participate in the Olympic Games, to determine the Olympic teams for each sport branch, etc.

198. The Registration Committee is composed of five members and three substitute members who have been a member in the association for at least ten years. They are elected by the General Assembly. This committee prepares a file for each member, registers their activities and keeps necessary documents, etc.

199. The High Counsel and Disciplinary Committee are composed of nine members and four substitute members who have been a member in the association for at least ten years. They are also elected by the General Assembly. This committee prepares an agenda and makes recommendations to the Executive Committee; the President of the Counsel attends the executive committee meetings but does not have the right to vote at this meeting. The President decides over disciplinary cases regarding members and performs other similar administrative functions.

200. Turkey is willing to host a Summer Olympic Games event in Istanbul. On 5 May 1992, with Law No. 3796, Law of Olympic Games, which will be held in Istanbul City, has been enacted by the Grand National Assembly.

201. As a unique example, throughout Europe, Turkey has set up a permanent Olympic Bid Committee and has passed the above-mentioned law stating that Istanbul shall bid for the Olympic Games until it is successful.

Istanbul has applied for the past four consecutive Summer Games bids (2000, 2004, 2008 and 2012), twice making it to the shortlist and having its best finish of fourth place in its bid for the 2008 Olympic Games. The Ataturk Olympic Stadium has already been built and stands ready to welcome the Games.

202. Turkey refrained from bidding for the 2016 Olympic Games and started to work for 2020. For the 2020 bids, the Olympic Bid Committee focused on the infrastructure and the organizational preparation for the Olympic Games. This last bid was defined as the strongest bid. Turkish Prime Minister announced Turkey's nomination on 7 July 2011 for the 2020 Summer Olympics. On 23 May 2012, the IOC shortlisted Istanbul. Along with Istanbul, Madrid and Tokyo were also in the shortlist. On 7 September 2013, an exhaustive ballot system was used in the final meeting which was held in Buenos Aires during the IOC's 125th Session. No city won over 50% of the votes in the first round, and Madrid and Istanbul were tied for second place. A run-off vote between these two cities was held to determine which would be eliminated. In the final vote, in a head-to-head contest between Tokyo and Istanbul, Tokyo was selected by sixty votes to thirty-six. After Madrid was eliminated, the European voters voted for Tokyo to make sure the 2024 Summer Olympics would return to the European continent. The disappointment was big. Since the 2024 and 2028 Summer Olympics host cities have already been announced by the IOC, Turkey's plans for 2032 have not been declared yet.

Chapter 2. Public Regulation

§1. Fundamental Rights

203. Fundamental rights have been secured by the Constitution of 1982. The Constitution recognizes all the basic human rights commonly found in liberal democratic constitutions, such as freedoms of speech, press, religion, association, assembly, travel and communications.

204. Freedom of association has been ruled under Article 33:

> Article 33 – Everyone has the right to form associations, or become a member of an association, or withdraw from membership without prior permission.
> No one shall be compelled to become or remain a member of an association.
> Freedom of association may be restricted only by law on the grounds of national security, public order, prevention of commission of crime, public morals, public health and protecting the freedoms of other individuals.

The formalities, conditions, and procedures to be applied in the exercise of freedom of association shall be prescribed by law.

Associations may be dissolved or suspended from activity by the decision of a judge in cases prescribed by law. However, where it is required for, and a delay constitutes a prejudice to, national security, public order, prevention of commission or continuation of a crime, or an arrest, an authority may be vested with power by law to suspend the association from activity. The decision of this authority shall be submitted for the approval of the judge having jurisdiction within twenty-four hours. The judge shall announce his/her decision within forty-eight hours; otherwise, this administrative decision shall be annulled automatically.

Provisions of the first paragraph shall not prevent imposition of restrictions on the rights of armed forces and security forces officials and civil servants to the extent that the duties of civil servants so require.

The provisions of this article shall also apply to foundations.

§2. Governmental Conditions and Permits

205. All the sports federations are free to regulate their own competition and eligibility conditions of athletes. The conditions of foreign players vary from federation to federation; in football, foreign players may not play at second and third leagues, and a club can sign a maximum of eight players in the first two leagues of basketball; however, there are some exceptions if the club is competing at EuroLeague. There are two types of licences in the matter of citizenship in sports legislation of Turkish Federations; first is licence for Turkish players and the second is licence for foreign players.

206. Law No. 4817 'Regarding Work Permits of Foreigners' exempts athletes from the obligation of obtaining a work permit. A Club which has signed an employment contract with a foreign athlete asks for registration from its federation. When the federation registers the athlete to the applicant Club, the federation sends this information to the Ministry of Labour and Social Security and also to the Ministry of Internal Affairs for residence permit.

207. These rules apply to all foreigners; there is no exception for European Union (EU) citizens.

208. At this point it would be useful to check EU and Turkey relations and its effect on working conditions of athletes in Turkey. Turkey is the only pluralist secular democracy in the Moslem world and has always attached great importance to developing its relations with other European countries. Historically, Turkish culture has had a profound impact over much of Eastern and Southern Europe.

209. Turkey's application to accede to the EU (previously the European Communities) was made on 14 April 1987. Turkey has been an associate member of the EU and its predecessors since the 1963 Ankara Agreement. After the ten founding members, Turkey was one of the first countries to become a member of the Council of Europe in 1949 and was also a founding member of the Organization for Economic Cooperation and Development in 1961 and the Organization for Security and Cooperation in Europe in 1973. It has also been an associate member of the Western EU since 1992. Turkey signed an Additional Protocol in 1970 and a Customs Union agreement with the EU in 1995, and it was officially recognized as a candidate for full membership on 12 December 1999 at the Helsinki Summit of the European Council. Negotiations started on 3 October 2005, and the process is likely to take several decades to complete. The membership bid has become a major controversy of the ongoing expansion of the EU.[4]

210. Since Turkey is not a full member of the EU, but has signed the Ankara Agreement and Additional Protocol, the legal situation with regard to the free movement rights of EU citizen players stands as a question mark.

211. The federations have not regulated a third type of licence for the EU citizen players.

212. However, there is a decision of the European Court of Justice (ECJ) which could force the federations to recognize a third type of licence for EU citizen players. A Turkish football player Nihat Kahveci was transferred to one of the La Liga Clubs of Spain, Real Sociedad de Fútbol, S.A.D and licensed as a foreign player by the Royal Spanish Football Federation (RFEF). Then, Mr Kahveci requested another licence which is only given to the EU citizen players from RFEF. RFEF rejected his request by stating that Turkey is not a member of the EU. However, Mr

4. At http://en.wikipedia.org/wiki/Accession_of_Turkey_to_the_European_Union, 20 Mar. 2009, www.ab.gov.tr, 31 Mar. 2024.

Kahveci carried the case to Spanish Courts, and finally the decision of ECJ came on 25 July 2008. ECJ referred to the *Kolpak*[5] and *Simutenkov*[6] cases. As Mr Kahveci was lawfully employed by a club established in an EU country, he was entitled under the Ankara Agreement and Additional Protocol between Turkey and EU not to be discriminated against in respect of his working conditions. Therefore, since he should have the same rights as EU nationals, the licence for EU nationals shall also be issued to him.[7]

213. The questions of what would be the reaction of Turkish sports federations if an EU citizen player requests a Turkish player licence or what would be the answer for the same request if it comes from a Spanish player still stands.

§3. Tort Law

I. Prevention of Violence in Sports Competitions

214. Two Super League Clubs had a game on 24 November 2004; the game was not ranked as a high-risked game; however, on that night, a fight at the grandstand began while the game was being played. Police forces were insufficient, and a 16-year-old boy Cihat Aktaş was stabbed and he died. This unfortunate incident has become a milestone in the Turkish sports world.

215. Although this was not the first death incident at a sports competition, the authorities were more alarmed because of the increasing violence in sports competitions throughout Europe. After this incident, solid measures were taken. The first reaction came from TFF because football was the most popular sports and so was violence in football.

216. A Stadium Security Committee has been established; the UEFA's Stadium and Security measures were taken as an example. All the stadiums in Turkey have been visited by a committee, and their infrastructural needs have been determined. The Regulation of Stadium Security set the criteria and asked the Clubs to fulfil the criteria gradually.

217. The progress in five years was unexpectedly successful. Today, before all the games in professional leagues, a liaison meeting is being held, all the professional clubs are subject to spot checks and also they are invited, at the beginning of all the seasons, to workshops. A protocol between the Ministry of Interior and TFF has been signed to better the police services for the football events, a fund has been established, and it is for service for the projects of the clubs on infrastructural maintenance and renovations, etc.

---

5. European Court of Justice, C-438/00, *Kolpak v. Deutscher Handballbund*, 8 May 2003.
6. European Court of Justice, C-265/03, *Simutenkov v. RFEF*, 12 Apr. 2005.
7. European Court of Justice, C-152/08, *Nihat Kahveci v. RFEF*, 25 Jul. 2008.

218. Turkey has already been a signing party to the European Convention on Spectator Violence[8] of the European Council. On 7 May 2004, Law No. 5149, the Law Regarding the Prevention of Violence and Disorderliness in Sport Competition, entered into force. Between 2004 and 2011, the imperfections were detected, and a new law was prepared. On 31 March 2011, a law was published on the Official Bulletin.

219. According to Law No. 6222, the City Security Committee was established. The committee is defined under Article 4 of the Law as:

> The Establishment of City and Town Security Committees
> Article 4 – (1) City Security Committee h is composed of under the presidency of the governor or deputy governor of the city and representatives of the city mayor, gendarmerie headquarters, police department, general directorate of sports, city health department, city education department, related sports federation, amateur sports confederation, a lawyer who is appointed by the governor, at least two representatives from the board members of the Clubs who are in charge of spectator relations and other related public organization.
> (2) Town Security Committees, is composed of under the presidency of the officer in charge of provincial district (town) and representatives of the same governmental bodies set forth in City Security Committees, a lawyer who is appointed by the officer in charge of provincial district, press and other related public organizations.

220. The obligations and functioning of the City Security Committee have been detailed in the Regulation Regarding the Application of Law No. 6222 which entered into force on 22 December 2012. The Committee shall take all the necessary measures in order to prevent the violence and the cheering in bad or racist language, to organize the police forces that will be on duty at the competitions, etc.

221. In Article 8, Fan Associations and in Article 9, Club Representative Responsible for Fans are defined. According to Article 9, each Club shall declare a number of fans who will be responsible for the spectators' behaviour at the competition. The Fan Representatives will help the authorities in preventing violence or cheering in bad or racist language. However, neither the law nor the regulation did clarify or detail how the representatives will help the authorities.

222. In practice, Law No. 6222's most working part is the City Security Committees; these Committees meet regularly and take necessary measures in order to prevent violence.

---

8. European Convention on Spectator Violence, Date of Council of Ministers' Decision: 23 Jul. 1990 No. 676, Official Bulletin Date: 26 Aug. 1990.

223. Under Article 5(4), electronic ticket is introduced to the system. In this article, a card is defined for the ones who want to watch a sporting event. This card shall bear all the identity information of the spectator. The application of this article was postponed until 24 January 2014.

224. In the same Article, installation of security cameras is also an obligation for all stadiums and other sport venues. A face identification system is going to be used to determine the exact spectator who breaks the law.

225. Under Article 5(7), the Clubs are obligated to build two rooms with a capacity of twenty people. The rooms are called 'control rooms'. These control rooms will be used by the police to keep the law-breaking spectators under control.

226. Manipulating game results has also been amended in Law No. 6222. Severe imprisonment sanctions were enacted. However, on 10 December 2011, these sanctions were reduced.

227. Article 11, having the title 'Match Fixing and Incentive Payment', does not bear a definition of this crime; it instead summarizes the crime as:

> A person who manipulates game results by making payment or other kinds of benefit shall be punished with imprisonment from one to three years and fined up to twenty days of monetary penalty. The person who receives the payment or other kinds of benefit shall be decided as the accomplice to the crime and shall be punished same. The act shall be evaluated as crime even parties just agree on payment or other benefits.

228. As it can clearly be understood from the wording, even an attempt is found to be enough for evaluating it as crime.

229. In the following paragraphs of the article, other actors of the crime are defined:

> (2) The ones who are aware of the agreement on manipulating game results and contribute to the realization of this agreement shall also be punished as stated in the first paragraph.

230. According to Article 11(3), attempt to this crime is defined. If someone offers or promises any kind of benefit for manipulating game results, however, if the parties cannot agree, then this act is deemed as an attempt to the crime of manipulating game results.

231. The aggravating circumstances are listed as if this crime is committed by a public officer or someone from the sports federation or club's members or representatives or establishing an organization to commit this crime or to manipulate betting. In case the crime is committed by one of these four options, then the punishment shall be increased by half. The only mitigating circumstance is in the event of 'incentive payments'. The most important change in this new Law is the sole authority of courts of law and public prosecutors. In Law No. 5149, some of the monetary fines were decided by the city or town security committees and these fines were classified as administrative fines. With Law No. 6222, the person who is accused of breaking this law does have the chance to be judged in front of courts of law.

232. On 4 July 2019, with Law No. 7182, some amendments have been made. Some of the important amendments made in the definition of 'Sporting area': The definition has been broadened; the places where spectators gather before, during and after the game have been accepted as 'sporting area'. So, any violation made at the places where spectators gather before, during and after the game will be deemed as it is made at the stadium. The police would have the right to body search without any further permission at these sporting areas. We can say the Law gave more power to police and defined severe sanctions to any violation of the spectators.

II. Gambling

233. Betting in sports is legal, but it is really restricted by law. Betting was first regulated by Law No. 7258 in 1958, Law Regarding Betting and Gambling over Football and other Sports Games. By this Law, an organization was founded under the supervision of the Ministry of Youth and Sports. The name of this organization is Spor Toto. Until 2008, Spor Toto Organization had two games: the first is Toto and the second is İddaa. Toto is designed for football, and it is the oldest game focused on football game results. However, İddaa is new and can be played for several sports.

In 2008, a new law was enacted; it is Law No. 5738 Law Fixed-Odds and Peri Mutual Betting Games in Sports to be organized by Private Law Legal Persons. With this Law, online betting websites were founded, but only five websites are legally authorized by Spor Toto Organization. They are bilyoner.com, nesine.com, misli.com, oley.com, tuttur.com, birebin.com. Other websites which offer bets in sports are illegal.

§4. Tax

234. The Turkish direct taxation system consists of two main taxes: income tax and corporate tax. An individual is subject to the income tax on his/her income and earnings, in contrast to a company, which is subject to corporate tax on its income and earnings.[9]

9. At www.gib.gov.tr/index.php?id=469, 12 Sep. 2008.

I. Taxation of Clubs

235. In Turkey, sports clubs are established either as associations or as incorporated companies. According to Article 7, subparagraph 8 of the Corporate Tax Law, the incorporated companies that are only in the sports business are exempt from corporate tax. Under normal circumstances, the incomes derived from sporting activities are not subject to corporate tax.

236. However, this exemption does not cover the business enterprises that are owned by sports clubs. Therefore, if the clubs have business enterprises, for example, official stores selling shirts, shoes and posters of clubs, those shall be subject to corporate tax. Therefore, the clubs choose to continue this kind of business by establishing new incorporated or limited companies.

II. VAT Liability

237. Sport clubs are liable for the VAT from their incomes, for example, gate revenues, broadcasting incomes and advertisement incomes. The rate of the VAT is 18%.

238. The VAT of the costs relating to the income is subtracted from the calculated VAT. The final amount is declared and paid to the relevant tax office.

III. Stamp Duty Liability

239. The contracts that are signed between the clubs and the sportsmen are subject to a 7.5% stamp duty. Clubs declare the amount, and they are liable to pay this tax to the tax office.

IV. Taxation of Sportsmen

240. Since a sportsman is an individual, the taxation of a sportsman is subject to Income Tax Law (ITL) No. 193.

241. Article 61 of the ITL, Definition of Fee, clearly states:

> Definition of Fee: Article 61 – Fee is an amount of money or a property which can be measured by money given to a working person for his/her services …
> Below stated payment shall also be considered as fee …
> 6. Transfer fees, payments or other benefits made to sportsman.

242. Therefore, any sportsman who has income from his sporting activity in Turkey is subject to income tax. In the law, professional or amateur sports have not been stated individually; the main criterion is having an income from the sporting activity. Moreover, the term 'income' is not specified; transfer fee, premiums, bonuses and so forth will be subject to taxation.[10]

243. In general, residency is the criterion in determining tax liability for individuals. This criterion requires that an individual who has his/her place of residence in Turkey is liable to pay tax for his/her worldwide income (unlimited liability). Any person who remains in Turkey for more than six months in a calendar year is assumed a resident of Turkey. However, foreigners who stay in Turkey for six months or more for a specific job or business or particular purposes that are specified in the ITL are not treated as residents, and, therefore, unlimited tax liability does not apply to them.

244. In addition to the residency criterion, within a limited scope, the nationality criterion also applies. Regardless of their residency status, Turkish citizens who live abroad and work for the government or a governmental institution or company whose headquarters is in Turkey are considered unlimited liable taxpayers. Accordingly, they are subject to income tax on their worldwide income.

245. Non-residents are liable to pay tax only on their income derived from sources in Turkey (limited liability). For tax purposes, it is especially important to determine in what circumstances income is deemed to be derived in Turkey.

246. To sum up, all sportsmen (regardless of their citizenship) who fulfil the residency criterion shall be liable to pay tax. However, to avoid double taxation, the treaties between Turkey and other countries shall be applicable to the taxpayer sportsman.

247. Article 29 of the ITL excludes tax liability from incomes such as bonuses and awards that are given to amateur sportsmen:

> Article 29 – Below listed incentive bonuses and awards shall be exempt from income taxation:
>
> …
>
> 3. Bonuses and awards paid to amateur sportsmen who have participated in sports competitions.

248. The exemption stated under Article 29 can only be applied to 'amateur' players.[11] The bonuses and awards that are paid to professional players are taxable.

249. There is another exemption stated under Article 23:

> Article 23 – The fees given below shall be exempted from income tax:
>
> …

---

10. S. Kızılot, *Gelir Vergisi Kanunu Uygulaması* (Ankara: Yaklasım Yayınları, 1989), 1243 et seq.
11. S. Kızılot, *Gelir Vergisi Kanunu Uygulaması* (Ankara: Yaklasım Yayınları, 1989), 444 et seq.

15. The fees which are paid to national amateur sportsman in the business enterprises employing hundred or less workers would be that of one worker, and for those employing more than hundred workers would be that of two workers. (Not to exceed two times of the minimum wage declared by the government.)

250. The objective of this article could be seen as an incentive to the business enterprises that employ amateur sportsman. There are two criteria: first is the limitation of amateur sportsmen workers, and second is the limitation of the fees that are paid thereto.[12]

251. On 5 December 2019, with Law No. 7194, a new regime for sportsman taxation was accepted by the Turkish Grand National Assembly:

Provisional Article 72 –

1. Until the date 31.12.2023, income tax deduction shall be done from the fees or other incomes which are deemed as fee from the rates given below;
   a. Sports branches which has 'league system'
      1. For the top league 20%,
      2. For the leagues under the top league % 15,
      3. For other leagues 10%,
   b. The payments in the sports branches that has no 'league system' and the payments which are done to the national team players for their participation 5%
2. Other deductions stated under Article 94 shall not be applied. Yearly basis declaration shall not be given, in case a declaration is given because of other incomes, these incomes shall not be included.

252. With the 311 No. Income Tax Bulletin, which was published on 27 May 2020, the professional sportsman was also held liable to income tax. This was something the community was waiting; the tax rates are quite high and individuals who are having low incomes are also subject to income tax, but professional players were not. For the employment contracts signed after 1 November 2019, the professional sportsmen are liable to pay income tax.

§5. Sports Justice

253. In Turkey, two different laws give the authority to regulate sports. The first is Law Decree Law (Executive Order) No. 638, Regarding Organization and Duties of Ministry of Youth and Sports, and the second is Law No. 5894, Law of Establishment and Objectives of TFF.

12. M.C. Yatkın, *Türkiye'de Sporcuların Vergilendirilmesi* (Ankara: Atılım Universitesi Yayınları, 2006), 63 et seq.

254. Although the Ministry has the general authority to regulate all sporting activity in Turkey, football is exempted from this authority by its law.

255. Moreover, according to Additional Article 9 of Law No. 3289, the federations that fulfil the criteria set forth in said article shall gain financial and administrative autonomy.

256. Since the dispute resolution system of TFF has been explained under the 'TFF' topic, jurisdiction of other federations will be explained.

257. As it comes to dispute resolution between the clubs and players, general courts of law have the jurisdiction.

I. Appeals Committee of the General Directorate

258. In Law No. 3289, the Appeals Committee is defined. The by-law of the Appeals Committee regulates the establishment, organization and procedures of the Appeals Committee of the General Directorate.

259. The Appeals Committee is composed of seven members and seven substitute members. Five of the seven members shall be lawyers, and the remaining two members shall be scholars, managers or technical directors in the sports world. The members are appointed by the Minister with the proposal of the General Director, and they serve for four years.

260. The decisions made by the federations may be appealed to the Appeals Committee of the General Directorate. The Appeals Committee examines and renders the final decisions upon the appeals lodged by the related parties against the decisions of the federation's Executive Committees with respect to disputes raised between federation and clubs; federation and referees; federation and technical directors, coaches, and managers; clubs and technical directors and coaches; clubs and sportsmen; and clubs and clubs; and the appeals lodged against the decisions of the Disciplinary Committees.

261. The Appeals Committee is independent while performing its duty. Unless the members resign or are deemed to be resigned, new members shall not be appointed. The substitute member in line shall be appointed when a member is discharged for any reason.

262. The Appeals Committee shall decide on an appeals application as fully accepted, partially accepted, rejected or rendered as a new decision on the appealed decision.

263. While rendering its decision, the Appeals Committee takes into consideration Law No. 3289, the rules of the relevant federation and its international association, the procedural law and equity. The decisions of the Appeals Committee are final. The decisions of the Appeals Committee shall not be challenged before any administrative body or court of law. Therefore, for the disputes that are mentioned in the law, the Appeals Committee jurisdiction constitutes a form of 'mandatory arbitration'. In the dispute resolution procedure, the Appeals Committee has exclusive jurisdiction, and its decisions cannot be challenged before the courts of law. However, the articles of procedural law relating to commentary of the decision, coram vobis[13] or renewal of trial are reserved.

264. The application shall be made by either a sportsman or the club or their lawyers. A petition and bank receipt certifying that the application fee has been deposited to the General Directorate's bank account are sufficient for the application. After the preliminary examination, if the application procedure has been made according to the by-law, the petition of the claimant is sent to the respondent. The respondent has ten days to reply to the claimant's petition. When the exchange of petitions procedure is completed, the Appeals Committee decides over the case. Under normal circumstances, the examination of the case is on file. If the Appeals Committee deems it necessary, it may schedule a hearing. The Appeals Committee shall decide over a case within three months.

265. When the Appeals Committee renders a decision over a case, the decision shall be applied by the federation immediately.

266. Under normal circumstances, the execution of the Disciplinary Committees' or Executive Committees' decision does not stay because of appeal. However, upon demand, the Appeals Committee may give a 'stay of execution' decision on the appealed decision.

13. Coram vobis is a legal writ issued by a court acting in its capacity as a Court of Equity to correct a previous error 'of the most fundamental character' to 'achieve justice' where 'no other remedy' is available.

Part II. Sports and Employment

§1. LABOUR LAW

I. Introduction

267. According to most of the legislations throughout Europe, professional players' contracts are subject to labour laws. On the contrary, in Turkish legislation, sportsmen are excluded from the Labour Code.[14]

268. Since there is no difference between physical, artistic, technical or scientific activities, all kinds of labour can be subject to an employment contract; thus, professional players' contracts can also be considered as an employment contract. In Article 393 of the Code of Obligations, an employment contract is defined as:

> An individual employment contract is a contract whereby the employee is obligated to perform work in the employer's service for either a fixed or an indefinite period of time, and the employer is obligated to pay wages based either on time periods or on the work performed.

269. There have been several discussions by scholars about the legal character of professional players' contracts.

270. Some of the scholars argue that although these contracts are excluded from the Labour Code, the players are the employees of the clubs and some rights, such as the right to strike, should be granted to players. Another group argues that since the wages are astronomically high, players are 'entrepreneurs'. However, the criterion of being paid an astronomically high wage should not lead us to such a conclusion, especially when we consider how wages vary among players in different sport branches and leagues. The Turkish Supreme Court also defined the contract as an employment contract.[15]

---

14. Labour Code, Law No. 4857, entered into force on 22 May 2003, 'Exceptions' heading Art. 4/g.
15. The Tenth Civil Chamber of Supreme Court, 24 Jan. 1974, Docket No. 1974/199, Decision No. 1974/1274.

II. Labour Union, Collective Bargaining, Strike and Lockout Rights

271. The Turkish Constitution states in the following articles that:

> Article 51 – Employees and employers have the right to form labour unions, employers' associations, and higher organizations, without obtaining permission, and they also possess the right to become a member of a union and to freely withdraw from membership, in order to safeguard and develop their economic and social rights and the interests of their members in their labour relations. No one shall be forced to become a member of a union or to withdraw from membership … .
> Article 53 – Workers and employers have the right to conclude collective bargaining agreements in order to regulate reciprocally their economic and social position and conditions of work … .
> Article 54 – Workers have the right to strike if a dispute arises during the collective bargaining process. The procedures and conditions governing the exercise of this right and the employer's recourse to a lockout, the scope of both actions, and the exceptions to which they are subject shall be regulated by law … .

272. According to Article 2 of the Union's Law, in order to establish a union, one shall be either a labourer or employer. In Article 21 of said law, a labourer who may not be a member of a union is listed, and a sportsman is not mentioned in this article. Thus, since sportsmen are deemed labourers under the Code of Obligations, they are eligible to establish or to be members of a union.

273. However, the Union's Law was adopted in principle to establish a union according to the lines of business. The lines of businesses are listed in the law; however, there is no special line for sportsmen or clubs. We are of the opinion that sportsmen and sports clubs should be considered under the 'general business' line.[16]

274. Regarding the Collective Bargaining Strike and Lockout Law, sportsmen and clubs having the right to establish a union shall also have the rights to collective bargaining, strike and lockout.

275. As we have clearly stated, there are no legal barriers to the rights to establish unions or collective bargaining, strike and lockout; however, currently, there has not been any union established either by sportsmen or by clubs.

276. There are several reasons for not being able to establish a union by sportsmen or clubs. The first and most important reason is that sportsmen are not well educated, and they are ignorant of their rights. There is only one association for sportsmen, the Professional Football Players Association. Being the leading sports

16. By stating such 'general business' line, the lawmaker's aim is to ensure that new business lines fall into the scope of the Union's Law.

branch, football players have this association; however, the association is not working effectively. Sportsmen are the weak party in sports business in Turkey. Therefore, clubs do not consider establishing a union for themselves.

277. In 1960s, a Turkish football player, şükrü Gülesin, wanted to establish a union for the players as he had seen in Italy. However, the members of the union were so low in number that it could not last very long. After the coop in 1980, the union was closed. Two other unions were also established later for not only football players but also other sports men. Finally, in 2012, another union only for football players was established. However, not all unions could become effective.

§2. UNIFORM CONTRACTS

278. 'Freedom of contract' is the main principle under both common-law and continental-law systems. It is the underpinning of the theory of laissez-faire economics and justifies it as a benefit to society.[17]

279. In simple words: 'Freedom of contract' is the idea that individuals should be free to bargain among themselves the terms of their own contracts, without government interference.

280. This principle is the outcome of a liberalization period that began in the nineteenth century. However, effects of World Wars I and II changed opinions about freedom of contract. Economic improvements, changes in the roles of governments in economic life, population growth and new types of commerce brought new perspectives to the 'freedom of contract' principle. Pre-printed uniform contracts entered into commercial life.[18]

281. In Turkey, the first pre-printed uniform contracts were used in the service sector. Big department stores, which have a dominant position in the market, began to offer pre-printed uniform contracts for their clients who wanted to make payments in instalments. Then credit card contracts entered into commercial life and others followed. The party that is in the dominant position makes the 'offer' with the pre-printed contract; by signing the contract, the client makes the 'acceptance'; then the contract is concluded. In this contractual relation, the client has no opportunity to discuss any article of the pre-printed contract. For this reason, the application of the 'freedom of contract' principle in such contracts has become doubtful. However, these pre-printed uniform contracts were prepared to meet the need of a high-speed, growing commercial world.

---

17. Dr E. Younkins, *Freedom to Contract*, http://www.quebecoislibre.org/younkins25.html, 31 Mar. 2024.
18. H. Ayrancı, 'Sözlesme Kurma Zorunlulu¢u', *Ankara Üniversitesi Hukuk Fakültesi Dergisi* (2003), 229–252.

282. Therefore, the authorities tend to accept that these contracts do not affect the 'freedom of contract' principle, as the parties concluding such contracts are willing to do so, and there is a freedom in the beginning phase. In addition, they argue that two main articles of the Code of Obligation should be applied in such contracts: Articles 26 and 27.

283. Article 26 of the Code of Obligations states:

> The terms of a contract may be freely determined within the limits of the law. Clauses that deviate from those prescribed by law are admissible only where the law does not prescribe mandatory forms of wording or where deviation from the legally prescribed terms would contravene public policy, morality or rights of personal privacy.

284. Article 27 states:

> A contract is void if its terms are impossible, unlawful or immoral.
> However, where the defect pertains only to certain terms of a contract, those terms alone are void unless there is a cause to assume that the contract would not have been concluded without them.

285. As a conclusion, pre-printed uniform contracts do not interfere with the 'freedom of contract' principle; however, judicial bodies have a tendency to interpret such contracts in favour of the weaker party.

286. When a sports federation's uniform contract is compared with the above-mentioned various types of uniform contracts, it is clear that it has different characteristics. Parties are free to agree to any terms and include any conditions that are not against the regulations of the federation or the basic principles of law in these contracts. The core idea of a mandatory pre-printed uniform contract is to create a 'fill-in-the-blanks' type contract in order to ensure the essential elements of a contract are being covered.

287. It is a fact that the professional sportsmen who play in the leagues other than the top league of their country are more numerous than the ones who are playing in the top league. Unfortunately, this majority needs more legal assistance than the top league sportsmen. Since their talents are limited, their profession and service are more open to abuse.

288. In the regulations of TFF, Turkish Basketball Federation, Turkish Volleyball Federation and Turkish Handball Federation, it is obligatory to sign a uniform contract between the sportsmen and the clubs.

289. In order to register the sportsmen to the clubs, the federations request from the clubs a notarized list of authorized signatures of the club representatives and a notarized declaration of each sportsman that he/she is willing to sign a contract with this club, containing the signature of the player; this notarized document will be used for signing of the contract. By requesting notarized signatures and such declaration, federations try to prevent any denials of signature that might be brought at the later stages of the contract's validity period.

290. For the individual sports, signing a contract is not compulsory. Federations give permission for contracts between the sportsmen and the clubs and request only that the parties register these contracts at the federation. Unfortunately, individual sport branches have not achieved the team sports level or in popularity. However, in our opinion, signing a contract between the parties should be compulsory in order to protect the sportsmen.

§3. Social Security

291. As stated above, since the professional sportsmen are paid by the clubs in return for their service, their contracts are employment contracts as defined in the Code of Obligations. According to Article 4 of the Social Security Law No. 5510, the person who is being paid in return for their service shall be deemed as insured.

292. Thus, we can see in the regulations of the sports federations that social security rights have been recognized and the clubs are obligated to take necessary measures. While registering the players, most of the federations request a document certifying that the sportsmen are insured in compliance with the Social Security Law.

Part III. Doping and Sports

§1. Introduction

293. Etymologically, the word 'doping' is derived from the words 'doop' or 'dope'. The word doping was first used in 1903 in England, and from 1931, the word 'stimulant' replaced the word 'doping'.

294. The first proposal to do research studies on doping was made in 1960 in Rome at an international Congress that was being held during the Rome Olympic Games.

295. In 1963, the Council of Europe gave a definition of doping:

> Doping means to make use of physiological substances in immoderate quantity or abnormal method from healthy people whose only aim is to obtain an artificial increase of the performance during the competition.

296. In this meeting of the Council of Europe, Turkey also contributed by giving a definition of doping as 'a pharmacologic stimulant that enhances performance'.

297. Another milestone is the foundation of the World Anti-doping Agency (WADA). WADA was established on 10 November 1999 in Lausanne to promote and coordinate the fight against doping in sport internationally.

298. In the WADA Code 2009 version, doping has been defined in Article 1 as:

> Doping is defined as the occurrence of one or more of the anti-doping rule violations set forth in Article 2.1 through Article 2.8 of the Code.

299. The articles mentioned in the definition are: the presence of a prohibited substance or its metabolites or markers, use or attempted use, refusing or failing without compelling justification to submit a sample collection, violation of applicable requirements regarding athlete availability for out-of-competition testing, any combination of three missed tests, tampering or attempted tampering with any part of doping, possession of a prohibited substance, trafficking or attempted trafficking in any prohibited substance, administration or attempted administration to any athlete in-competition/out-of-competition of any prohibited method or prohibited substance.

300. In the WADA Code, all the stakeholders and the governments are also obligated to participate in the fight against doping.

301. Under Article 22 of the Code, the governments' commitment is required to fight against doping by being a signing party of the Copenhagen Declaration on Anti-doping in Sport of the United Nations Educational, Scientific and Cultural Organization (UNESCO) on 3 March 2003. By ratifying, accepting, approving or acceding to the UNESCO Convention, the governments undertake to fulfil the requirements that are set forth in the Convention and the Code. The deadline for the fulfilment of these requirements is 1 January 2010. Any party failing to do so shall face ineligibility to bid for events, major events or organizations and additional consequences.[19]

§2. Doping and Turkey

302. As the anti-doping movement began and accelerated in the world, Turkey was following this movement with little steps. On the contrary to world anti-doping systems, Turkey took the road beginning from the last step. Instead of establishing an anti-doping organization, Turkey founded a laboratory, followed by a specific event.

303. Naim Suleimanov[20] was a Turkish-originated Bulgarian citizen. While on a trip to the World Cup final in Melbourne in 1986, Suleimanov escaped from a Bulgarian delegate to Turkey by secretly going to the Turkish Embassy in Melbourne. He resurfaced in Turkey and applied for citizenship. He also changed his name from the Bulgarian Suleimanov to the Turkish Süleymanoğlu. He flew to London and was brought to Turkey via the special plane of the Turkish Prime Minister. A battle over which country he would represent in the 1988 Seoul Olympics arose. The Bulgarian government demanded and received USD 1,000,000 from Turkey to allow him to compete for Turkey. The then Prime Minister of Turkey, Mr Turgut Ozal, believed in him and invested such money. However, in 1987, his first world championship could not be registered because there was no doping control system in Turkey. After this event, by the rule of the Prime Minister in 1989, the Turkish Doping Control Centre was established under Hacettepe University.

19. World Anti-doping Code, 2009, Art. 22.
20. Naim Süleymano¢lu (born 23 Jan. 1967 in Bulgaria), formerly known as Naim Suleimanov, is a Turkish World and Olympic Champion in weightlifting. He won three Olympic Championships, seven World Championships, and six European Championships and earned forty-six world records; http://en.wikipedia.org/wiki/Naim_Suleymanoglu, 3 Jan. 2009.

304. The Centre was accredited in 2003 by IOC and WADA. Despite its short history, the Centre became one of the leading centres throughout Europe and the Middle East.

305. On 26 August 2003, the General Directorate of Youth and Sports published on the Official Bulletin the Anti-doping Regulation. In the regulation, doping is defined as:

> Definitions: Article 4 –
> … Doping in Sports: To give sportsman the doping substances which are in the pharmacologic classifications and using doping methods or the usage of these methods by sportsman.

306. In the Regulation, the Hacettepe University's Turkish Doping Control Centre is intended as the sole authoritative doping control centre for the tests.

307. In the following articles, the doping control procedures are detailed. The prohibited substances list is being updated on a yearly basis.

308. If the doping control test result is positive in a professional sports branch, the sportsman will be punished according to the related federation's Disciplinary Regulation. If the sports branch is amateur, then the sportsman shall be punished according to the General Directorate's Disciplinary Regulation for Amateur Sports.

309. All sports federations that have a Disciplinary Regulation have included the doping offence in their regulations.

310. However, because of the lack of education and awareness about doping and its damages to health, positive test results are still happening.

311. Unfortunately, in some branches of sports, the usage of doping substances and methods is common.

312. The two most famous international doping cases of Turkey are the Turkish Weightlifting Federation's case and Süreyya Ayhan Kop's[21] case.

313. After the repeated positive results of the doping control tests of the Turkish delegation, the Turkish Weightlifting Federation was fined USD 100,000 and suspended from all international competitions until 3 May 2006, following a series of anti-doping violations on 15 November 2005 by the International Weightlifting Federation.

314. The International Weightlifting Federation's Executive Committee sanctioned the Turkish federation for 'bringing the sport of weightlifting into disrepute'.

---

21. Süreyya Ayhan Kop (born 6 Sep. 1978 in çankırı, Turkey) is a middle-distance track runner and is a European record holder. In November 2007, she was banned from athletics for four years.

315. After this decision, the Turkish Halter Federation concentrated their attention on anti-doping studies.

316. Süreyya Ayhan Kop was the hope of Turkey for the athletics branch in the 2004 Athens Summer Olympic Games. Until 2004, Turkey had only one bronze medal and was expecting a gold medal from Kop. However, a short time before the Olympic Games, Süreyya Ayhan Kop declared that she was injured during her training in Germany and would not be able to participate in the 2004 Summer Olympic Games. After a while, Süreyya Ayhan was punished by the International Association of Athletics Federation (IAAF) with a two-year ban because of not cooperating with the IAAF officials. Although the sample tested negative, she was banned for two years.

317. While the athlete was training in the United States for the 2008 Summer Olympics, she was tested again. This time, the test results were positive; two prohibited substances were detected in her sample. The Turkish Athletics Federation's Disciplinary Committee banned her for life since this was her second offence. However, the Appeals Committee of the General Directorate annulled this decision and gave her a four-year ban. The Appeals Committee stated in its decision that in the previous infringement, she had not tested positive, and since she tested positive for the first time, the punishment shall be a two-year ban from all competitions and another two-year ban because she committed this offence in a foreign country.

318. However, the athlete appealed this decision before CAS and IAAF. In the end, CAS decided that this was her second offence and decided that a life time ban should be applicable.

319. Süreyya Ayhan Kop appealed the case to the Swiss Federal Code. She argued that the basic principle of '*reformation in peius*' has not been applied to her case. She also argued that her two doping offences originated from two different behaviours; therefore, she had to be punished separately. However, the Swiss Federal Court rejected Mrs Kop's appeal.

320. The best practice of an anti-doping fight belongs to TFF.[22]

321. On 25 August 2008, the Anti-doping Regulation of TFF entered into force. The regulation has been amended several times, and the harmonization of the regulation with FIFA's and UEFA's Anti-doping Regulations and the WADA Code is ensured.

22. T. Atasü & R. Güner, 'Türkiye Futbol Federasyonu Dopingle Mücadele çalısmaları', in *Doping ve Futbolda Performans Arttırma Yöntemleri*, ed. T. Atasü (Istanbul: Turkish Football Federation, 2005), 173–177.

322. From 1993 to 2003, all the samples that were collected from the players were sent to the accredited Cologne Doping Control Centre to be analysed; as of the 2003–2004 football season, all the samples are being analysed at the Turkish Doping Control Centre.

323. Between 1993 and 2004, of the 1,696 samples collected from professional players, 24 tested positive. The ratio of the collected samples and positive test results is 1.41%.[23]

324. In the 2004–2005 football season, 460 samples were collected.

325. In the 2005–2006 season, 456 samples were collected.

326. In the 2006–2007 season, 812 samples during competition and eighteen out-of-competition samples were collected. Four tested positive out of 812 samples. The ratio of the collected samples and positive test results is 0.49%.

327. In the 2007–2008 season, 1,017 samples during competition and 25 out-of-competition samples were collected.

328. In the 2008–2009 season, as of 1 March 2009, 744 samples during competition were collected and one of them tested positive. As of 11 January 2009, 64 out-of-competition samples were collected and none of them tested positive.

329. As it can be clearly seen from the statistics, doping usage in football is not common in Turkey.

330. TFF's Anti-doping Committee not only operates the sample collection procedure but also educates the clubs and players in order to prevent them from using prohibited substances by sending publications to the clubs and organizing seminars on doping.

I. Turkish Anti-doping Commission

331. Turkey adopted the Anti-doping Convention of the European Council dated 16 November 1989 on 12 October 1993.[24] Also, at the World Conference Doping in Sports, which was held on 5 March 2003 in Copenhagen, the Minister of the State

23. The players who were subjected to a doping control test are reported and published on the website of the TFF, www.tff.org. The test results were not indicated in several reports. Therefore, we could not give the test result information.
24. Anti-doping Convention, date of Council of Ministers' Decision: 8 Sep. 1993, No. 93/4813, Official Bulletin dated 12 Oct. 1993.

and TUMOK signed the Copenhagen Declaration. Turkey is also a party to UNESCO's International Convention against Doping in Sport, which was signed on 19 October 2005 in Paris.[25]

332. On 24 May 2011, a protocol between the General Directorate of Youth and Sports and TUMOK was established. With this protocol, the General Directorate assigned its authority to do all the anti-doping activities to TUMOK.

333. Turkish NOC has established a commission and named it as Turkish Anti-doping Commission. The commission has been recognized by WADA, and as of November 2011, Turkey became one of the Code-compliant countries.

334. The Commission is composed of five members. The criteria to become a member are: holding a university degree, having specialized in the field of law or sports and practised them for at least five years.

335. The Commission enacted the Turkish Anti-doping Code in September 2011. The Code is adopted from Model Rules of WADA. All the sports federations accepted the authority of the Turkish Anti-doping Commission.

336. Finally, Turkey fulfilled its duties set forth in Conventions; however, there are still some issues that need to be dealt with. Unfortunately, limiting the sale of doping pharmaceuticals is still a problem. Also, dietary supplements are freely being sold in Turkey. The upcoming steps must be taken towards legislating sale and consumption of those substances.

25. Law No. 5721, Law Regarding the Approval of the International Convention against Doping in Sport, Official Bulletin dated 18 Dec. 2007, No. 26734.

Part IV. Sports and Commerce

Chapter 1. General Issues

337. The concept of commercialization of sports is quite new. Since football is the most popular and economically improving sport in Turkey, commercial transactions were first set up in this branch of sport. Therefore, the following topics will be focused on football.

§1. Media and Television Rights

338. Broadcasting is distribution of audio and/or video signals that transmit programmes to an audience.[26]

339. First, the facts of centralizing the broadcasting system will be briefly explained and then the legal structure will be given.

I. Television Broadcasting

A. *Centralizing the Broadcasting System*

340. Under the prior terms, the clubs had the right to do their own broadcasting contracts of the games that were played at home. In this system, big clubs have the opportunity to sell all their games' broadcasting rights in a season; however, the smaller clubs have the chance to sell their three or four home games' rights when the big clubs come to play with them. The difference between the economic powers of the clubs is increasing.

341. TFF centralized[27] the broadcasting rights of the Super League by an amendment to the Broadcasting Regulation. The principle of distributing the revenues was also decided by TFF's Executive Committee. TFF signed a contract with Cine 5 channel on 25 June 1997 for three years, transferring the entire broadcasting rights of the Super League.

26. At http://en.wikipedia.org, 13 Feb. 2009.
27. The 'centralized system' is to market all the broadcasting rights of the participants of a sports organization from one source.

342. At the signing date, there were no major problems because the same TV channel had individual broadcasting contracts with the three big clubs: Galatasaray, Beşiktaş and Fenerbahçe. They seemed to be satisfied with the distribution of the revenues. However, after the 1996–1997 season began, Beşiktaş FC's and Fenerbahçe FC's individual broadcasting contracts ended. Other TV channels that were uncomfortable with the centralized system tried to challenge it. Beşiktaş and Fenerbahçe FCs signed new individual broadcasting contracts with channels other than Cine 5. According to the Broadcasting Regulation of TFF, the clubs needed to submit the contracts to TFF. TFF did not approve these individual contracts, stating that they were conflicting with the centralized system. After this refusal decision of TFF, these two clubs appealed before the Appeals Committee.

343. In Beşiktaş FC's case, the Appeals Committee stated in its decision that the individual contract validity period shall not be changed by the new Broadcasting Regulation. However, it also stated that the centralized system and the contract with Cine 5 channel are also valid and that Beşiktaş FC was receiving revenues; therefore, the contract between TFF and Cine 5 shall also be recognized and binding for the appellant club.

344. Fenerbahçe FC had an individual contract with Cine 5; therefore, the club declared clearly that they did not want to be a part of the centralized system. In its claim, the Fenerbahçe FC requested TFF to approve its broadcasting rights of home games in advance. The Appeals Committee stated in its decision that the claim of the appellant club was keeping the broadcasting rights of their home games. This claim was interpreted to mean that Fenerbahçe FC indirectly accepted the centralized system for away games. Since the authority to decide on Fenerbahçe FC's approval request belonged to TFF's Executive Committee, the Appeals Committee rejected Fenerbahçe FC's appeal.

345. In both decisions, the Appeals Committee could not satisfy the parties with the legal grounds of their decision. However, it tried to maintain the centralized system and gave its decision on the grounds of an *ex aequo et bono* principle.

346. The same dispute has also been carried to civil courts, and the courts decided that being the obligatory legal representative of the clubs, TFF is entitled to sign such a contract and its affiliates shall also recognize it.

347. After Cine 5 contract, several other contracts have been signed, and the most recent contract was signed between TFF and one of the leading pay TV channels, Digiturk.

348. It has been twelve years since the centralized system was established by TFF. In the past years, the most common complaint from the big clubs was from the distribution principle. In the latest version of the statute of TFF, Article 74, Authorization for Broadcasting, states in subparagraph 8 that:

The TFF shall be entitled to draw up specifications, hold tenders and sign agreements on behalf of clubs with regard to licenses for broadcasting league matches on TV and radio. The TFF may consult with the Clubs' Union.

349. For now, once this statute enters into force, the dispute over the centralized system will be over for an indefinite period of time.

B. Legal Aspects of Broadcasting Rights in Football

350. In Law No. 5894, Establishment and Objectives of TFF, Article 13 states:

> Broadcasting and VIP stand arrangements
> **ARTICLE 13** (1) The TFF Executive Board shall be exclusively entitled to broadcast all the football matches in the territory of the Republic of Turkey on TV, radio, the Internet and via all other similar sound and data carriers, and to organize and plan such broadcasts.
> (2) The above-said power particularly encompasses the marketing of the TFF's broadcasting rights centrally and the distribution of the proceeds derived from such rights to Member clubs in such manner as may be decided by the relevant bodies of the TFF.
> (3) Encrypted broadcasting of national team's matches is prohibited.

351. The term 'broadcasting' is used for all kinds of media, such as television, radio and other means of broadcasting (Internet and mobile rights).

352. The statutes of TFF detail the question of how the centralized broadcasting system works:

> Article 74 Authorization for Broadcasting
>
> 1. The Executive Committee of the TFF shall be exclusively entitled to grant the right to broadcast matches on television, radio, the Internet and all other similar sound and data carriers, and to organize and plan such broadcasts.
> 2. (Added by the decision of Congress at 12.6.2009) The above-said power encompasses particularly the marketing of the TFF's broadcasting rights centrally and the distribution of the proceeds derived from such rights to Member clubs in such manner as may be decided by the relevant bodies of the TFF.
> 3. When exercising the said power, the Executive Committee shall prioritize the interests of Turkish football, clubs and the TFF.
> 4. Encrypted broadcasting of national teams is prohibited.
> 5. Mobile rights shall be regulated exclusively by the Executive Committee of the TFF.
> 6. Any agreement signed between a club and a broadcasting company shall be subject to the TFF's supervision and approval. Any such agreement not approved by the TFF shall not be binding on the TFF. No match shall be

broadcast on TV, radio, the Internet and all other similar sound and data carriers, unless the required license therefore has been received from the TFF.

7. The rules and procedures governing the cooperation among the General Directorate of Youth and Sports, the Provincial Directorates and Provincial Offices regarding the broadcasting of matches shall be laid down in a Protocol Regarding the Utilization of Sports Facilities and Services of Personnel.
8. The rules and procedures regarding the broadcasting of matches, and the rights that may be given to and the sanctions that may be imposed on broadcasting companies and clubs shall be specified in the Broadcasting Regulations to be drawn up by the Executive Committee.
9. The TFF shall be entitled to draw up specifications, hold tenders and sign agreements on behalf of clubs with regard to licenses for broadcasting league matches on TV and radio. The TFF may consult with the Clubs' Union regarding the broadcasting rights of the Super League.
10. The tender for broadcasting rights shall be held not earlier than one year and not later than six months prior to the expiry of the existing broadcasting license.

353. The most important novelty is to add Clubs' Union to the bidding process and consults thereto. In 2010, the broadcasting rights of the Super League were held for four years. TFF prepared the bid specifications with Clubs' Union and finally the broadcasting rights of Turkish Super League were sold to Digiturk. One year later, the conditions of sale were negotiated again with Digiturk, and at the end of the negotiations, Digiturk accepted to pay USD 321 million for five years.

354. In 2017, another bid opened for the broadcasting rights of the Turkish Super League. This time the Turkish First League was also added to the package. Digiturk offered USD 500 million for five years for the rights to live broadcasting of two leagues' games, international sale right of Turkish Super League games, radio broadcasting rights of these two leagues, title sponsorship right of the First League and mobile rights thereof. Finally, Digiturk won the bid, and by this number the Turkish Super League was listed as 6th, following Premier League of the United Kingdom, La Liga of Spain, Seria A of Italy, Ligue 1 of France and Bundesliga of Germany.

355. TFF regulated the broadcasting with its Broadcasting Regulation. The principles of sale of broadcasting rights at lower leagues, whose rights have not been centralized, have been set by the Broadcasting Regulation. Moreover, some infrastructural criteria are set for the clubs whose rights have been sold.

C. The Legal Nature of Broadcasting Contracts

356. The broadcasting of the league games via television can be done by a contract signed between TFF and the broadcasting company or an agency. The legal nature of the contract shall be determined briefly as a mixed contract covering the purchase and lease agreement elements. The shooting, recording and broadcasting of the games can be done with the permit given by the organizing authority that is acting as a licensor. One party of the contract is the organizer (e.g., clubs, related international or national federation, a football player for his/her jubilee game), and the other party is either a broadcasting company or an agency.

357. The object of the contract is based on the permit given by the organizer to shoot, record and broadcast one football game or a group of games (e.g., league or cup championship) in a determined type of broadcasting technology (e.g., antenna, satellite, cable, pay TV or Internet) for a determined period of time and geographical territory.

358. If the organizer undertakes to prevent the broadcasting of the same event with the same kind of broadcasting methods to the other broadcasting companies, the contracting company will have the 'exclusivity' of that event.

D. Owner of the Broadcasting Rights

359. TFF has classified the ownership of the broadcasting rights and the authority to manage thereof in its Broadcasting Regulation.

360. If TFF does not commercialize the broadcasting rights of a league, then these clubs shall have the authority to sell their own rights.[28]

361. If TFF does not commercialize the radio transmission of a league, then these clubs shall have the authority to sell their own rights.[29]

362. The rights of the jubilee game belong to the player who retires from his/her footballing activity.[30] The player is free to sign a contract with the broadcasting company.

363. The federation is exclusively authorized to sign broadcasting contracts on behalf of the clubs.[31]

364. The rights other than specified above belong to the clubs. Those clubs must sign a written contract and submit it to TFF for approval.

28. TFF Broadcasting Regulation, Art. 3.
29. TFF Broadcasting Regulation, Art. 3.
30. TFF Broadcasting Regulation, Art. 5.
31. TFF Broadcasting Regulation, Art. 3.

365. Restriction of the rights that belong to the clubs is against the law. The law gives the exclusive authority to TFF's Executive Board 'to broadcast', 'to regulate the broadcast' and 'to plan' the said right. However, most scholars are of the idea that this given authority should not be interpreted as TFF being the legal representative of the clubs.[32]

366. However, in the decisions of the civil courts, the court decided that since the whole authority is given in Article 1 of Law No. 3813 to TFF, TFF is entitled to centralize the broadcasting system and can act on behalf of clubs.[33]

E. Centralized Broadcasting System and Turkish Competition Law

367. Both the Law and the regulations of TFF required an 'Association of Undertakings' regarding the centralized broadcasting system. The members of this association are TFF and clubs that are competing in TFF's organizations. The centralized broadcasting system affects the competition both vertically (TFF by being the 'sole' authority) and horizontally (economic relations between the broadcasting companies in the market and the association of undertakings and members thereof).

368. The members of the union are in an 'undertaking' according to the Law of Protection of Competition, Article 3/IV:

> Definitions Article 3 –
> … Undertaking: Natural and legal persons who produce market and sell goods or services in the market, and units which can decide independently and do constitute an economic whole ….

369. The Court of Jurisdictional Disputes defined the Clubs as a commercial entity and the broadcasting activity of the games via television and radio as a commercial activity. Moreover, it stated that each football league whose members are the clubs competing for the championship of that league forms an 'association of undertakings'.

370. By organizing the professional and amateur leagues, ensuring the National Team to compete in international tournaments, and signing sponsorship, advertisement and broadcasting contracts, TFF produces and sells goods or services in the market and joins the economic life. Therefore, TFF is also an 'undertaking' under the Law of Protection of Competition.

---

32. H. Aker, *Futbol Karşılaşmalarına İlişkin Yayın Haklarının Hukuki Niteliği ve Rekabet Hukuku Açısından Yayın Haklarının Merkezi Pazarlaması* (Ankara: Ankara Üniversitesi Hukuk Fakültesi Dergisi, 2006), 1–46.
33. Istanbul Sixth Commercial Court, Docket No. 1996/760, Decision No. 1997/625, which is also approved by the Supreme Court by its eleventh Civil Law Chamber on 8 Jun. 1998.

371. There is no doubt that TFF is not only an undertaking but also serves for the public. While serving for the public, TFF also generates an economic activity by marketing its products. In this respect, TFF not only acts as a representative of the clubs but also manages the whole process by itself. TFF sets rules for the market and requires the clubs and the participants of the market to obey these rules. The contracting broadcasting company makes payment to TFF. After deducting 10% of the payment, TFF disburses the income to the Clubs. In a decision of the Turkish Competition Authority, TFF was also defined as an undertaking.[34]

372. In order to investigate the association of undertakings whose members are TFF and the clubs, the markets that the competition is due shall be defined. The Turkish Competition Authority sets 'the broadcasting rights market of Turkish Super League clubs' and 'the image market of the Turkish Super League games'. The Authority also stated in its decision that the 'television broadcasting market' has been affected indirectly.[35]

373. According to the Turkish Competition Authority, in the market of broadcasting rights, in the image market, the contracting broadcasting companies form a monopoly.[36] Therefore, the contracting broadcasting companies have been punished by an administrative fine because of their abuse of a dominant position.[37] TFF has not been subjected to the investigation process because of their exclusive authority given by the power of law.

374. After the decisions of the Turkish Competition Authority, various measures have been taken by TFF and implemented in their bid specifications and regulations; for example, the contracting party shall sell a short footage covering all the important positions of the game to the other broadcasting companies in return of a reasonable price. This footage shall be prepared and distributed to the demanding companies within forty-five minutes after the game.

II. Radio Broadcasting

375. As mentioned above, according to Article 4 of TFF Broadcasting Regulation, all broadcasting rights are centralized and TFF has the exclusive right to market these rights.

---

34. Decision No. 01-07/62-19, date of Decision: 6 Feb. 2001, Official Bulletin dated 14 Jul. 2003, No. 25168.
35. Decision No. 99-46/500-316, date of Decision: 11 Oct. 1999, Official Bulletin dated 3 Apr. 2001, No. 24362; Decision No. 01-51/514-126, date of Decision: 23 Oct. 2001, Official Bulletin dated 2 Dec. 2002, No. 24954.
36. TFF Law and Broadcasting Regulation.
37. Decision No. 99-46/500-316, date of Decision: 11 Oct. 1999, Official Bulletin dated 3 Apr. 2001, S. 24362 (Cine 5); Decision No. 01-07/62-19, date of Decision: 6 Feb. 2001, Official Bulletin dated 14 Jul. 2003, No. 25168 (TELEON).

376. For the 2007–2008 season, TFF centralized the radio broadcasting rights of the Turkish Super League and signed a contract with a radio broadcasting company, Alem FM, on 3 September 2007.

377. In 2017, TFF formed a package for the bid of Turkish Super League broadcasting rights. The radio broadcasting rights of the Turkish Super League and First League were added to the said package. Digiturk won the bid and held the radio right of the two leagues.

§2. Sponsoring

378. In today's business climate, as the marketing processes among companies are getting more complicated and tougher, the companies have to introduce themselves and their brands in a way to compete with other competitors, so the companies must be creative when communicating their message and must be familiar with all marketing techniques in order to publicize their brands.

379. In Turkey, the first sponsoring agreements were seen in cultural activities. Sponsors were used to invest in film festivals, particularly movies. Sponsoring in sports events is quite new in Turkey.

380. As it has always been in Europe, football was the first branch in sports that attracted the sponsors' attention. In the beginning, solely the sports equipment companies were the sponsors of FCs. For the past couple of decades, brands other than sport equipment companies have been sponsoring in football.

381. Today, the national football team, therefore TFF, is the leading federation among others in means of receiving the largest piece from the sponsors' cake. After football, basketball and volleyball followed in sponsorships in team sports; tennis and swimming have the most sponsors in individual sports.

382. As the government recognized the valuable contribution of the sponsorship agreements in sports, it made several amendments to several laws and tried to encourage the companies to sign more sponsoring agreements in sports in 2004.

383. This operation was completed with three major amendments in three laws.

384. An additional article was added to Law No. 3289, Law Regarding Organization and Duties of General Directorate of Youth and Sports:

> Award and Sponsorship Additional Article 3 – … The real and legal persons may sponsor the following events;
>
> a. National and international sports events which have been stated in the General Directorate's yearly activity programme,

b. Excluding the transfer fee of the sportsman, any official sporting activity which has been stated in the yearly activity programme of the related sports federation,
c. To build or to give maintenance service for the facilities which are belong to governmental organizations or federations or clubs,
d. To supply sport equipment to the federations or clubs,
e. All the expenses of individual licensed sportsman who are authorized to participate in national or international sports events,
f. Turkish National Olympic Committee and Paralympics' Committee's services,

Individual or team sports athletes, sports clubs, shall accept advertising agreements for the national or international organizations, in accordance with the rules which are going to be set by the General Directorate.
The expenses for the sporting activities, sportsman, sports clubs, federations or facilities shall be allowed directly by the sponsors or shall be deposited to the bank accounts thereof.

The title, advertising and broadcasting rights might be transferred to the sponsors unless it is not violating the national or international federation's sponsorship regulation.
The principles and procedures regarding sponsoring and advertising shall be defined in the Regulation of General Directorate.

385. Related article in ITL:

Other Discounts Article 89 – Following discounts shall be done while determining the tax base value;
...
8. 50% of the professional sports branches and 100% of the amateur sports branches sponsoring expenses in relation with the Law Regarding Organization and Duties of General Directorate of Youth and Sports and Law of Establishment and Objectives of Turkish Football Federation.

386. Related article in the Corporate Tax Law:

Other Discounts Article 10 – Following discount shall be done while determining the tax base value;
...
b) 50% of the professional sports branches and 100% of the amateur sports branches sponsoring expenses in relation with the Law Regarding Organization and Duties of General Directorate of Youth and Sports and Law of Establishment and Objectives of Turkish Football Federation.

387. Without any doubt, these three amendments increased the brands' attention in sports. The General Directorate also published its Regulation for Sponsorship in the Official Bulletin dated 16 June 2004. In this regulation, the General Directorate set the principles of a sponsorship agreement and the other procedures to be followed by the parties of the agreement. Both the General Directorate and TFF published sample sponsorship agreements on their websites, and they try to motive their affiliates to do sponsorship agreements.

§3. IMAGE RIGHTS

388. The importance of image rights is constantly increasing due to the change and development of promotion and advertising in today's world that makes it necessary for big enterprises to enter into agreements with famous sportsmen in order to associate their products or services with them. The public's favourable disposition towards these famous sportsmen will hopefully make them prefer and buy the specific products or services because they will associate them with the sportsmen.[38]

389. In Turkish theory, image rights are evaluated under 'personality rights'. The elements of personality rights or the content thereof have been developed by the jurisdictions in time. Image, voice, likeness, shirt number, name, nicknames, signature, caricature and other 'indicia' of an individual might be considered under personality rights.

390. The personality right has been ruled under the Turkish Civil Code.

I. Protection of Personality

A. Against Waiver and Extreme Restrictions

391. Article 23 – No person may waive his/her rights and capacity to act freely even if it is in the least degree.

Neither a person may waive his/her freedom nor may any one impose restrictions on a person contrary to the laws and ethics.

II. Against Assault

A. Basic Principle

392. Article 24 – The person subject to violation of his/her personal rights may claim protection from the judge against the individuals who made the violation.

Each violation against personal rights is considered contrary to the laws unless the consent of the person whose personal right is damaged is based on any one of the reasons related to private or public interest and use of authorization conferred upon by the laws.

38. D.Z. Konstantinos, 'Image Rights', ISDE – IEB Master in International Sports Law Program lesson notes (Madrid, May 2007).

B. Lawsuits

393. Article 25 – The claimant may demand from the judge to take an action for prevention of violation, interception of such threat and determination of unlawful consequences of the violation even though it is discontinued.

In addition to such action, the claimant may also request publication or notification of the recovery or the judgment to the third parties.

Right of the claimant to demand compensation for physical and moral damages and to request the transfer of gains incurred from unlawful violation in his favour under the provisions stipulating performance of business without the requirement of proxy is hereby reserved.

Claim for compensation of moral damages may not be transferred unless it is accepted by the counterparty; also, it may not be transferred to the heirs by way of inheritance unless it is expressly declared by the testator.

The claimant may file an action in the probate court at his/her locality or at the settlement place of the defendant for the protection of his/her rights.

III. Rights Pertaining to Possession of a Name

A. Designation of a Name

394. Article 26 – The person who is subject to confusion in use of name may litigate in the competent court for establishment of his/her respective rights.

A person subject to unjust use of his/her name may claim discontinuation of such act; where the person is in default due to use of the name unjustifiably, then he/she may demand recovery of his/her tangible losses as well as indemnification of moral damages whichever the case may require.

395. Image rights in Turkey can be protected by reference to and use of the personality right, which is defined and ruled in the Turkish Civil Code. Without a doubt, image right is a personal and absolute right directly connected with one's personality right and being.

396. In Article 24/II, the violation against the personality right is exempted under the following three conditions: the consent of the individual, the reasons related to public interest and whether the authorization conferred by law is being exercised.

397. An individual may give consent by signing contracts about the usage of his/her personal rights or signing a simple waiver.

398. The most problematic condition, and the one open to interpretation, is the public interest exemption. Most personality rights violations are committed by the media, especially in the name of 'public interest', 'freedom of the press' and 'freedom of information'.

399. The right to inform is one of the *sine qua non* elements of freedom of the press. The Turkish Constitution also protects these rights under Article 28/II by stating: 'The State shall take the necessary measures to ensure the freedom of the press and freedom of information.' While exercising the right to inform, the image, voice or other personal information may be used, and this may inevitably cause a violation of the personality right of the individual. Therefore, if this information or news is not subject to one of the exempt conditions that are set forth in Article 24 of the Turkish Civil Code, there is no doubt that civil and/or criminal liability will be born.

400. The statute of the individual in society plays a major role in deciding if the right to inform is violating the personality right of the individual.

401. Statesmen, politicians, writers, artists, sportsmen, and scientists are the individuals who attract the attention of the public. Therefore, the information or the news directly or indirectly related to their profession shall not constitute a violation of the personality rights. However, when these people are subject to news that is not directly related to their profession but more related to their personal life, the courts decide on the specific news. Publishing intimate pictures of a football player shall constitute a violation of personality rights, whereas the publication of his and his girlfriend's pictures on the way to a restaurant shall be interpreted as information that attracts the public interest.

402. As it is stated under Article 25, the individual whose personality rights have been violated can bring lawsuits to the courts.

403. There are three kinds of lawsuits. The first is prevention of violation; this lawsuit can be filed before the violation. However, in this case, the claimant would have to prove that the danger of violation is in the near future and is serious. The second is interception of violation; this lawsuit can be filed while the violation is continuing. The claimant asks from the court to stop or terminate the violation. The third lawsuit is the determination of unlawful consequences of the violation; this lawsuit can be filed even after the violation has been finished. The claimant asks from the court to determine the effects of the violation.

404. There are also other ways to protect the individual if the violation has been done by a newspaper or any other type of media that is privately regulated under the Law of Press or the Law Regarding Regulation of Internet Publishing.

405. According to these laws, an individual may ask from the media to publish his/her 'answer' to the news or request a 'correction'. If the media refuses to publish the individual's answer or the correction, then several lawsuits can be filed against the media company.

406. In sports, especially in football, image rights play an important role when it comes to using players' images in advertising and gaming industry. Although there is no law about this subject, the common assumption is that the players' image rights transfer to clubs if only they are used in a club's advertising or gaming project as a part of the team.

§4. Property Rights

I. Protection of Trademarks

407. In Turkey, trademarks are protected by Industrial Property Law No: 6769. Article 3 of the law states:

> Persons Entitled to Protection
> Article 3 – (1) The protection conferred by this law is available to;
>
> a) Turkish citizens
> b) Real and legal persons who are domiciled or who have industrial or commercial establishments within the territory of the Turkish Republic,
> c) Persons who have application rights resulting from the terms of the Paris or the Agreement Establishing World Trade Organization dated 15/4/1994.
> d) In appropriate with the rule of reciprocity, citizens who belong to countries which protects Turkish Citizens' industrial property rights.

408. As it is clearly stated in Article 3, all real and legal persons are entitled to protection:

> Signs of Which a Trademark May Consist
> Article 4 – (1) A trademark, provided that it is capable of distinguishing the goods and services of one undertaking from the goods and services of other undertakings, may consist of all kinds of signs being represented graphically such as words, including personal names, designs, letters, numerals, shape of the goods or their packaging and similarly descriptive means capable of being published and reproduced by printing.
> Trademark may be registered along with the product or the packaging. However, the registration of the product or the packaging does not grant exclusive rights.

409. Contrary to other countries' trademark protection laws, the image of a real person or legal person shall not be registered as a trademark under Turkish law. Also, in Article 5, absolute grounds for refusal of a trademark application are listed:

> Absolute Grounds for Refusal for Registry of a Trademark
> Article 5 – (1) Following signs shall not be registered as a trademark:
>
> a. signs which do not conform with the provisions of Article 4,
> b. signs which do not have any distinguishing character,

c. trademarks identical or confusingly similar with a trademark registered earlier or with an earlier date of application for registration in respect of an identical or same type of product or services,
d. trademarks which consist exclusively of signs or indications which serve in trade to indicate the kind, characteristics, quality, intended purpose, value, geographical origin, or designate the time of production of the goods or of rendering of the service or other characteristics of goods or services,
e. trademarks which consist exclusively of signs and names used to distinguish specific groups of craftsmen, professionals or tradesmen or have become customary in the current and established practices of the trade,
f. signs containing the shape of the product which results from the nature of the good, which is necessary to obtain a technical result or which gives substantial value to the good,
g. trademarks which are of such a nature as to deceive the public, such as to the nature, quality, place of production or geographical origin of the goods and services,
h. trademarks which have not been authorised by the competent authorises and are to be refused pursuant to Article 6ter of the Paris Convention,
i. trademarks containing badges, emblems or escutcheons other than those covered by Article 6ter of the Paris Convention which have not been authorised by the competent authorises and are of particular historical and cultural public interest,
j. trademarks which have not been authorised by their owners, well known marks according to 6bis of the Paris Convention,
k. trademarks which contain religious symbols,
l. trademarks which contrary to public policy and to accepted principles of morality.

410. After a trademark has been registered, the applicant receives a 'Trademark Certificate of Registry'. A trademark is registered for a period of ten years from the date of filing of the application. Registration may be renewed for further periods of ten years.

411. After the registry, if, within a period of five years following the registration, a trademark has not been put to use without a justifiable reason or if the use has been suspended during an uninterrupted period of five years, the trademark shall be repealed.

412. Transferring or licensing of a trademark is possible under the Decree Law.

413. Severe sanctions shall be applicable in case of a trademark infringement, such as fines, imprisonment, closing down the undertaking for a period of time, or preventing an individual from practising any commercial activity.

414. Today in the sports world, most of the famous sportsmen have registered their names as a trademark. Moreover, clubs have also registered their logo, names, shirts and so forth.

§5. Unfair Competition

415. Unfair competition is regulated under the Turkish Commercial Code, Articles 54–63. The definition of unfair competition is stated in Article 54:

> Chapter Four
> A) In General I – Purpose and Principle – This article's purpose is to ensure honest and non-deformed competition on behalf of all the participants of economy.

416. In the following paragraphs, according to Article 55, some of the actions leading to unfair competition are listed. They are not *numerus clausus*. Therefore, any act or commercial practices that are against the spirit of competition in means of Article 54 are also classified as unfair competition acts, and they are prohibited by the law.

417. Some of the violations are: to denigrate another's goods, products, business or financial position; to give false or misleading information about themselves to others; causing confusion to consumers by adopting another's trademark or name; to obtain know-how or other commercial secrets by deceiving another's good faith.

418. Civil lawsuits may be filed against unfair competition; for example, determination of unfair competition, correcting the misleading statement and compensation for physical and moral damages.

419. Criminal lawsuits may be filed, and severe sanctions shall be applicable in a case of unfair competition, such as fines, imprisonment, closing down the undertaking for a period of time or preventing an individual from practising any commercial activity.

420. Thus, a famous sportsman could have recourse to the article by claiming that the exploitation of his fame and reputation, and in particular his name and/or image for commercial and financial purposes, constitutes illegal anticompetitive conduct.

Impact of COVID-19 on Sports in Turkey

421. The COVID-19 outbreak was officially recognized by the Turkish Government in March 2020. On 13 March 2020, TFF declared that the games will be played behind closed doors.

422. On 19 March 2020, President, Minister of Youth and Sports, Presidents of the Turkish Football, Volleyball and Basketball Federations met and declared that all the leagues have been postponed until further notice.

423. On 12 June 2020, Turkish Super League and First League resumed; for the lower leagues, only play-off stages had been played. On 29 July 2020, TFF announced that there will be no relegation from the Super League to First League. The 2020–2021 season played with twenty-one teams. However, TFF wants to return to the eighteen-team league system; therefore, the Super League will be played with twenty teams in the 2021–2022 season.

424. The Basketball Federation did not resume the leagues, declared the 2019–2020 season as ended and declared no relegation or promotion.

425. The Volleyball Federation also declared the leagues as ended and did not resume the games.

426. None of the Federations or Government declared any aid for the Clubs or the Players.

Annex I Law on the Establishment and Duties of the Turkish Football Federation

Law No. 5894 Enacted: 5 May 2009

Objective

ARTICLE 1 (1) The objective of this Law is to set out the principles and procedures regarding the establishment, organizational structure, duties and powers of the Turkish Football Federation, a self-governing association subject to private law, to conduct, organize and develop all kinds of football activities in accordance with the related national and international laws and also to represent Turkey in Turkey and abroad on subjects related to football.

Definitions and acronyms

ARTICLE 2 (1) The following terms used herein shall have the following meanings:

a. FIFA: Fédération Internationale de Football Association.
b. UEFA: Union of European Football Associations.
c. TFF: Turkish Football Federation.
d. Congress: The Congress of the Turkish Football Federation.
e. President: The President of the Turkish Football Federation.
f. Executive Board: The Executive Board of the Turkish Football Federation.
g. Emergency Committee: The Committee that takes decisions between two Executive Board meetings concerning the urgent matters,
h. Audit Committee: The Audit Committee of the Turkish Football Federation.
i. Disciplinary Committees: Committees that examine and sanction any disciplinary infringement or unsporting behaviour by any club or person in accordance with the Football Disciplinary Regulations drawn up by the Executive Board.
j. General Secretary: The General Secretary of the Turkish Football Federation.
k. General Secretariat: The General Secretariat of the Turkish Football Federation.
l. TFF Statutes: The regulatory arrangements adopted by the TFF Congress with respect to association football, the procedures and principles stipulated under this Law and all other matters concerning the enforcement of this Law.

m. Regulations: The regulatory arrangements adopted by the TFF Executive Board in accordance with and within the framework of the Statute.
n. Standing and Ad-Hoc Committees: The ancillary committees formed outside the central organization of the TFF to carry out the activities described under this Law.
o. Club Licensing Committee: The Committee which decides to issue a license to an applicant club or not, under the Club Licensing Regulations of the TFF.

Duties of the Turkish Football Federation

ARTICLE 3 (1) The duties of the Turkish Football Federation are as follows:

a. To organize, regulate and monitor all football activities within Turkey;
b. To promote the development and expansion of football throughout the country;
c. To ensure the proper implementation of the rules set by the governing bodies of FIFA and UEFA, set up all domestic regulations and represent Turkey abroad on subjects related to football;
d. To make plans, programs, arrangements and agreements of any kind related to football activities both domestically and abroad and to take the necessary measures to achieve successful results;
e. To organize and regulate competitions at all levels and take all necessary steps to ensure the admission and participation of its representative national and club teams in international competitions;
f. To observe the principles of loyalty, integrity and sportsmanship in accordance with the rules of Fair Play;
g. To ensure that its own members, clubs, football players, officials, managers, head coaches and trainers, medical staff, players' agents, match agents and all other related people comply with the statutes, regulations and directives set forth by FIFA, UEFA and the TFF as well as the decisions adopted by the competent organs and bodies of these governing bodies;
h. To fight against violence, match-fixing, illegal performance incentives, racism, doping and any kind of discrimination;
i. To provide both financial and in-kind support to amateur sports clubs, associations and including the sports associations for the disabled involved in football, with a view to improving the game of football.

(2) The organization, duties and powers of the TFF, the rules of procedure for the TFF organization, the responsibilities of the TFF's other central, domestic and overseas units, departments and offices as well as all other matters concerning the enforcement of this Law shall be set forth in accordance with both the TFF Statute, which will be adopted by the Congress in line with the statutes of both FIFA and UEFA, with which the TFF is affiliated, and take effect upon being published in the Official Gazette, and the regulations that will be drawn up by the Executive Board and, unless otherwise stipulated, take effect upon being announced on the official website of the TFF.

Organization

ARTICLE 4 –

1. The organization of the TFF shall be set out in the TFF Statutes.
2. The organization of the TFF shall be composed of its Head-office and both affiliated domestic and overseas offices. The Head-office of the TFF is in Ankara.
3. All football organizations in Turkey shall be legally subordinated to the TFF and their respective rights and responsibilities shall be described by the TFF Statutes and regulations.
4. TFF is a member of both FIFA and UEFA.
5. The central organization of the TFF shall consist of at least the following organs:
    a. Congress
    b. President
    c. Executive Board
    d. Emergency Committee
    e. Legal Committees
    f. Audit Committee
    g. General Secretary
6. The consultative and administrative units of TFF shall consist of the following bodies:
    a. General Secretariat
    b. Standing and Ad-Hoc Committees
7. The members of the TFF organs and committees shall either be appointed or elected in accordance with the TFF Statute.
8. Elections for all TFF organs shall be held by means of free and independent democratic procedures.

Legal committees of first instance

ARTICLE 5 (1) The legal committees of first instance of the TFF shall consist particularly of the following committees:

a. Dispute Resolution Committee.
b. Disciplinary Committees.
c. Club Licensing Committee.
d. Ethics Committee.

(2) (Annulled: Constitutional Court's decision dated 18/01/2018)
(3) TFF's regulations and any decision awarded by any one of the TFF legal committees of first instance shall be final and binding, if not appealed against within seven days following their promulgation or, in the latter case, the notification of the decision. No legal action may be taken against before any judicial body in the matters falling within the jurisdiction of the TFF legal committees of first instance or any decisions of the TFF legal committees of first instance.

(4) The composition, responsibilities, powers, rights, duties, and requirements for its members as well as the procedural rules for each of the TFF legal committees of first instance shall defined in the TFF Statute and the corresponding regulations.
(5) The individual members of the TFF legal committees of first instance shall be appointed as described in the TFF Statutes.
(6) No member of any of the TFF legal committees of first instance shall hold a seat on any other committee or organ of TFF or carry out a duty for a club or a private law legal entity which is a member of TFF at the same time. These members must execute their duties in complete independency and impartiality pursuant to their mandate at all times.

Arbitration Committee

ARTICLE 6 (1) The Arbitration Committee is an independent and impartial compulsory arbitration authority which is the top legal committee of TFF under the present Law and is also the legal body of last instance for disputes covered by the TFF Statutes and corresponding regulations.
(2) The Arbitration Committee exclusively and finally examines and decides over the decisions taken by any TFF organ or body, which has decision-making power given by the TFF Statutes and corresponding regulations. The time limit for appealing against any TFF regulation or any decision of any TFF organ before the Arbitration Committee is seven days following the promulgation of such regulation or, in the latter case, the notification of such decision.
(3) The composition, responsibilities, powers, rights and duties of the Arbitration Committee shall be described in the TFF Statutes and the corresponding regulations as well as the responsibilities, powers, rights, duties, and requirements for its members. The procedural rules for the Arbitration Committee shall be described by regulations to be issued by TFF.
(4) Any decision taken by the Arbitration Committee shall be final and binding for the relevant parties and no legal action may be taken against these decisions before any other judicial authorities.
(5) The members of the Arbitration Committee shall also be subject to paragraph 6 of Article 5 of this Law.

Audit Committee

ARTICLE 7 (1) The TFF's accounting books and financial position shall be audited by the Audit Committee that is elected by the Congress. A copy of the Audit Committee's report shall be distributed to the Congress delegates at least fifteen days before the date of the next Congress meeting and shall also be presented at the Congress meeting.

Revenues of the TFF

ARTICLE 8 (1) The revenue of the TFF shall arise from:

a. 15% royalty collected from clubs in relation to football betting games and fixed-odds betting games.
b. Application fees and fines.

c. 10% of the proceeds received by clubs from their matches that will be broadcast through TV, radio, the Internet or through any other similar data carrier and from any contract they have signed with any media company.
d. Revenues arising from sponsorship agreements signed by the TFF.
e. Revenues obtained from official and friendly National Team matches and remaining after all legally required deductions, as well as those proceeds derived from such matches broadcast on TV, radio, the Internet or via any other similar data carrier.
f. Registration and registration renewal fees, transfer levies, subscriptions and similar other fees collected from players and clubs affiliated with the TFF.
g. Proceeds derived from the TFF's fixed assets and from other activities such as the transfer, assignment, sale and lease of its real properties.
h. Income from all kinds of economic enterprises and corporations, whether established or invested in by the TFF.
i. Interest receipts.
j. Donations and grants.
k. Others.

Expenditures of the TFF

ARTICLE 9 (1) The TFF shall prepare its annual budget and incur any and all expenses that may be necessary to perform its duties hereunder in accordance with the TFF Statute.

Independent Audit

ARTICLE 10 (1) The TFF's financial statements and profit and loss accounts shall be audited on a yearly basis by an independent audit firm that has financial audit experience in the international sports industry.
(2) The audit reports shall be disclosed to the public after being reviewed at the TFF Congress.
(3) The Congress delegates shall be provided with a copy of the audit report prior to the Congress meeting in accordance with the relevant provisions in the TFF Statute.
(4) No audit firm shall provide financial audit services to the TFF for more than five consecutive years.

Tax exemption and priority of sums due to the TFF

ARTICLE 11 (1) Proceeds derived from matches and competitions organized in Turkey under the auspices of FIFA, UEFA and the TFF and under this Law as well as all other revenues of the TFF shall be exempt from taxes, duties and charges of any nature.
(2) The said tax exemption shall not cover the TFF's economic enterprises and those deductions required under both Income Law No. 193, enacted on 31 December 1960, and Corporate Income Law No. 5520, enacted on 13 June 2006.
(3) Fines imposed by the TFF on clubs in accordance with Article 15 of this Law shall first be deducted from the sums due by the TFF to such clubs, respectively.

Annex I

Club Licensing System

ARTICLE 12 (1) The TFF Executive Board shall set up regulations in accordance with the club licensing system regulations of FIFA and UEFA governing the participation of TFF clubs in the domestic competitions of TFF.

Broadcasting and VIP stand arrangements

ARTICLE 13 (1) The TFF Executive Board shall be exclusively entitled to broadcast all the football matches in the territory of the Republic of Turkey on TV, radio, the Internet and via all other similar sound and data carriers, and to organize and plan such broadcasts.
(2) The above-said power particularly encompasses the marketing of the TFF's broadcasting rights centrally and the distribution of the proceeds derived from such rights to Member clubs in such manner as may be decided by the relevant bodies of the TFF.
(3) Encrypted broadcasting of national team's matches is prohibited.
(4) (Annulled: Constitutional Court's decision dated 06.01.2011)
(5) The number of individuals who may have access to the VIP stands of any sports facility which the General Directorate of Youth and Sports has transferred or rented out to, or allocated for use for a limited time period by, sports clubs or public organisations or institutions under a protocol shall be decided by the related Provincial or District Directorate of Youth and Sports in line with the instructions of the General Directorate of Youth and Sports and the VIP stands of such sports facility shall be organized by the same Provincial or District Directorate. In the event of national teams' matches, these VIP stands shall be organized by the TFF.

Intellectual, industrial and commercial property rights

ARTICLE 14 (1) The ownership and the utilization rights of the trademarks, logos and similar intellectual and industrial property rights, which are used or will be used by the TFF, shall belong exclusively to the TFF. The existence of these rights does not prevent the TFF from registering such intellectual and industrial property rights to the Turkish Patent Institute and International Patent Offices.
(2) Any individual making public announcements, advertisements, promotional notices or carrying out other similar activities in a manner so as to give third parties the impression that he/she is a sponsor of the TFF despite the fact he/she is not, he/she shall be sanctioned under Turkish Code of Commerce No. 6762, enacted on 29 June 1956.

Sanctions

ARTICLE 15 (1) Disciplinary infringements and unsporting behaviors by any club or individual in any football match or activity and the penalties that shall be imposed on such club or individual shall be set out in a regulation drawn up by the Executive Board in accordance with the TFF Statute and in line with the relevant regulations of FIFA and UEFA.

Cancellation of Congress Decisions

ARTICLE 16 (1) An action for rescission can be filed against any decision taken at the TFF Congress in violation of the national law or the TFF Statute before the Civil Court of First Instance, where the TFF has its Head-office, within 30 days from the relevant meeting date.

The petty sessions procedure shall apply to such cases.

Leave

ARTICLE 17 (1) Any referee, representative, observer or a TFF Committee member, who holds a public office and has been assigned to a match which will be played on a business day or weekend, shall be deemed to have obtained official permission to be absent from his public duty throughout the term of such assignment, provided that his supervisor has been informed thereof.
(2) The time period of such assignment shall be fixed under the related regulations of the TFF.

Provisions applicable

ARTICLE 18 (1) Any regulation or directive issued by the TFF on the basis of this Law as well as practices regarding such regulation or directive can only and solely be appealed against before the Arbitration Committee.
(2) Matters not covered by this Law, the TFF Statute or other relevant regulations shall be governed by Associations Law No. 5253, enacted on 04 November 2004, and Turkish Civil Law No. 4721, enacted on 22 November 2002.

Provisions repealed

ARTICLE 19 (1) Law No. 3813 on the Establishment and Duties of the Turkish Football Federation, enacted on 17 June 1992, was repealed.

Organs, statute and regulations

TEMPORARY ARTICLE 1 (1) The organs of the TFF elected under Law 3813 shall hold office until the expiry of their respective terms of office.
(2) The existing Main Statute and regulations of the TFF and those provisions of the TFF Statute, which was adopted by the Congress on 06 June 2008, that are not in contravention of the present Law shall continue to be in effect until the TFF Statute and regulations adopted under the present Law take effect in full.
(3) Any amendments to be made in the TFF Statute in line with the present Law shall be decided at the next ordinary Congress meeting that will be held following the coming into force of the present Law.

Coming into force

ARTICLE 20 (1) The present Law shall come into force on the date it is published in the Official Gazette.

Execution

ARTICLE 21 (1) The provisions of the present Law shall be executed by the Council of Ministers.

Annex I

Annex II Statutes of the Turkish Football Federation

Definitions

The terms given below denote the following:

CAS (TAS):	Court of Arbitration for Sport in Lausanne, Switzerland.
Association:	A football Association recognized by and a Member of FIFA.
FIFA:	Fédération Internationale de Football Association.
Association Football:	The game controlled by FIFA and organized in accordance with the Laws of the Game.
Player:	A football player registered with an Association.
Congress:	The supreme organ of TFF.
Ordinary Courts:	State courts which hear public and private legal disputes.
IFAB:	The International Football Association Board responsible for altering and approving the Laws of the game.
Confederation:	A group of Associations recognized by FIFA and belonging to the same continent (or similar geographic area).
Club:	Direct or indirect Member of a football Association.
League:	An organization subordinate to an Association.
TFF:	Turkish Football Federation.
UEFA:	Union des Associations Européennes de Football.
Member:	A legal or real person that has been admitted into membership of TFF by the Congress.

Officials:	All board members, committee members, coaches, referees, assistant referees, coaches, attendants as well as other people responsible for technical, medical and administrative matters at FIFA, a Confederation, Association or Club.
Executive Committee:	The executive organ of TFF (abbreviation EXCO).

I GENERAL PROVISIONS

Article 1 Name, headquarters, legal form and insignia

1. The objective of these Statutes is to exclusively regulate the general principles and the procedures of the establishment, organisation, duties and authorisations of the Turkish Football Association which is a self-governing organisation. These Statutes cover the execution, organisation and development of all football activities in Turkey in accordance with national and international rules.
2. Pursuant to these Statutes, the TFF is the sole legal entity authorised to organise and regulate the sport of football at national level and to represent Turkey domestically and internationally for matters relating to football.
3. (Amended by the decision of Congress at 12.6.2009) The headquarters of the Turkish Football Federation is in Ankara.
4. The abbreviation of the Turkish Football Federation is TFF.
5. The TFF is a Member of FIFA since 1923 and of UEFA since 1962.
6. The TFF's logo is as shown in the Annex to these Statutes.

Article 2 Objectives

1. The objectives of TFF are:
   a. To organise, regulate and monitor all football activities within Turkey;
   b. To promote the development and expansion of football throughout the country;
   c. To ensure the proper implementation of rules set by the governing bodies of FIFA and UEFA and to set up all domestic regulations as well as to represent Turkey abroad on subjects related to football;
   d. To make any plans, programs, arrangements and agreements related to football activities both domestically and abroad as well as to take the necessary measures to achieve successful results;
   e. To organise and to regulate its own competitions at all levels and to take all necessary steps to ensure the admission and participation of its national teams and club teams in international competitions;
   f. To ensure that its own members, clubs, football players, officials, managers, technical directors and trainers, physiotherapists, players' agents,

match agents and all other related people comply with the statutes, regulations and directives set forth by FIFA, UEFA and TFF as well as the decisions taken by the competent organs and bodies of these football governing bodies;

g. (Amended by the decision of Congress at 12.6.2009) To fight against violence, match fixing, illegal performance incentives, racism, doping and any kind of discrimination;
h. To conduct and regulate all kinds of football activities, ensure the improvement and promotion of the game of football throughout Turkey, and adopt and carry out all such arrangements and decisions as TFF may think proper in the light of unifying, educational, cultural and humanitarian values, particularly through youth and development programmes;
i. To ensure that any and all national and international football rules and regulations in force are applied, and represent Turkey abroad in all football-related matters;
j. (Amended by the decision of Congress at 29.06.2011) To observe the principles of loyalty, integrity and sportsmanship in accordance with the rules of Fair Play and the Code of Ethics of both FIFA and UEFA;
k. To comply with the Laws of the Game as laid down by the International Football Association Board ('IFAB') as well as any other laws of the game as issued by FIFA and UEFA;
l. To abide by the Statutes, regulations and decisions of FIFA and UEFA;
m. (Amended by the decision of Congress at 01.06.2019) To recognise the jurisdiction of the judicial bodies described in the related articles of the Statutes of FIFA and UEFA and the jurisdiction of the Court of Arbitration for Sport ('CAS');
n. To protect the interests of all parties involved in football;
o. To ensure that all illegal methods or practices which might jeopardise the integrity of matches or competitions or give rise to abuse of football are prevented;
p. (Added by the decision of Congress at 12.6.2009) To provide both financial and in-kind support to amateur sports clubs, associations and including the sports associations for the disabled involved in football, with a view to improving the game of football.

2. In order to achieve and implement these aforementioned objectives, TFF shall enact all necessary regulations, directives and agreements, and shall ensure that the competent organs and bodies of TFF take all appropriate decisions to implement these objectives and all such regulations, directives and agreements in accordance with the present Statutes.

Article 3 Neutrality and non-discrimination

1. TFF is neutral in all matters.
2. All kind of discrimination against a country, private person or groups of people is strictly prohibited and punishable by suspension or expulsion.

Annex II

Article 4 Promoting friendly relations

1. TFF shall promote friendly relations between its Members, Clubs, Officials and Players and in society for humanitarian objectives.
2. Every person and organisation involved in the game of football is obliged to observe the Statutes, regulations, directives and decisions of FIFA, UEFA as well as the principles of loyalty, integrity and sportsmanship in accordance with the principles of Fair Play.
3. (Amended by the Congress at 29.06.2011) Unless it is not prohibited by Law, TFF shall provide the necessary institutional means to resolve any internal dispute that may arise between its members, clubs, referees, players, head coaches and coaches, player representatives, medical stuff, match agents in Turkey.

Article 5 Players and other individuals of football

1. The status of Players and the provisions for their transfer shall be regulated by the Executive Committee of TFF in accordance with the current FIFA Regulations for the Status and Transfer of Players.
2. Players must be registered in accordance with the corresponding regulations approved by the Executive Committee of TFF.
3. The Executive Committee may further regulate the registration of any other individual taking an active role within football (e.g., Head Coaches, Medical staff, Referees player representatives, match agents etc.) through the TFF Registration regulations.

Article 6 Laws of the Game

TFF and each of its Members play association football in compliance with the Laws of the Game issued by IFAB. Only IFAB may regulate and alter the Laws of the Game.

Article 7 Conduct of members of TFF organs/bodies and Officials

The members of any TFF organ or body as well as any Official of TFF must observe the Statutes, regulations, directives and decisions of FIFA, UEFA and TFF as well as the Code of Ethics of FIFA, if applicable in their activities as well as the principles of loyalty, integrity and sportsmanship in accordance with the principles of Fair Play.

II MEMBERSHIP

Article 8 Admission, suspension and expulsion

1. The Congress shall decide whether to admit, suspend or expel a Member.

2. Membership is terminated by resignation or expulsion. Loss of membership does not relieve the Member from its financial obligations towards FIFA, UEFA, TFF or other Members of TFF, but leads to cancellation of all rights in relation to TFF.

Article 9 Members of TFF

The Members of TFF are:

a. Clubs of the Turkish Professional Leagues;
b. Amateur Sports Clubs Confederation;
c. Professional Footballers' Association;
d. Turkish Football Trainers' Association;
e. Turkish Association of Active Football Referees and Observers;
f. Disabled sports associations involved in Football;
g. Individuals who are serving on the Executive Committee of FIFA or UEFA;
h. Individuals who served actively on the committees of FIFA or UEFA for a period of at least 10 years;
i. Individuals who served as President of the Turkish Football Federation in person;
j. Other individuals admitted into membership by the Congress.

Article 10 Procedure for application

1. The procedure for application and the membership conditions are defined in the Regulations governing the affiliation of TFF members approved by the Executive Committee.
2. The Executive Committee shall recommend to the Congress either to admit or not to admit an applicant. The applicant may state the reasons for its application to the Congress. The Congress has the full discretion for its decision.
3. A new Member shall acquire membership rights and duties with immediate effect.

Article 11 Admission

1. Any legal or real person wishing to become a Member of TFF shall apply to the General Secretariat of TFF in writing.
2. The application of any legal person must be accompanied by the following mandatory items:
   a. A copy of the applicant's by-laws, articles of incorporation or such other regulations depending on its legal status;
   b. (Amended by the Congress on 29.06.2011) A declaration signed by the duly authorised representatives of the applicant and stating that the applicant shall always comply with the Statutes, regulations and decisions of

FIFA, UEFA and TFF and shall recognise the CAS/TAS as specified in their Statutes and shall ensure that these are also respected by its own Members, Clubs, Officials and Players;
   c. A declaration that it will comply with the Laws of the Game, the Futsal and Beach Soccer Laws of the Game in force;
   d. A written declaration that the applicant is based and registered in Turkey;
   e. A declaration that the applicant's legal composition enables it to make decisions independently of any external entity;
   f. A list of the applicant's duly authorised representatives and authorized signatories and the list of authorized signatures;
   g. A notarised copy of the minutes of the applicant's latest congress;
   h. A declaration that it undertakes to organise or participate in friendly matches only with the prior consent of TFF.
3. The application of any real person must be accompanied by the following mandatory items:
   a. A declaration that he/she will always comply with the Statutes, regulations and decisions of FIFA, UEFA and TFF as well as the FIFA Code of Ethics and will recognise the CAS/TAS as specified in their Statutes;
   b. Providing written proof to be Turkish citizen;
   c. Providing written proof having either served as member of the FIFA or UEFA Emergency Committee, served as member of a FIFA or UEFA committee for at least ten years or having served as President of TFF.
4. A legal person admitted to membership shall be represented by only one (1) delegate at the Congress unless otherwise decided by the Congress.

Article 12 Members' rights

1. The Members of TFF have the following rights:
   a. to take part in the TFF's Congress, to be informed of its agenda in advance, to be called to the Congress within the prescribed period of time and to exercise their voting rights;
   b. to draw up proposals for inclusion in the agenda of the Ordinary Congress;
   c. to be informed of the affairs of the TFF through the official bodies of the TFF;
   d. to take part in competitions, if possible, and/or other sports activities organized by TFF;
   e. to exercise all other rights vested in TFF's membership by virtue of the Statutes and regulations of the TFF;
2. The exercise of these rights is subject to other provisions in these Statutes and the applicable regulations.

Article 13 Members' obligations

1. The Members of TFF have the following obligations:
   a. to comply strictly with the Statutes, regulations, directives and decisions of FIFA, UEFA and TFF and ensure that these are also fully respected by its own members at all times through a mandatory provision to be included in its own statutes or incorporation provisions or any other regulations;
   b. to ensure that its decision-making bodies are formed through free elections;
   c. to take part in competitions and other sports activities organised by TFF exclusively for sports clubs affiliated to TFF;
   d. to pay its membership subscriptions and the annual fees;
   e. to comply by the Laws of the Game issued by IFAB and with the Laws of the Game of Futsal and Beach Soccer both issued by the FIFA and ensure that these are also complied with by its members at all times;
   f. to recognise the jurisdiction of the Court of Arbitration for Sport (CAS) in Lausanne (Switzerland) for international disputes as specified in the relevant provisions of FIFA and UEFA Statutes;
   g. (Amended by the decision of Congress at 29.06.2011) Unless it is not prohibited by Law, to apply to the Arbitration Committee as a last instance at all disputes of national dimension arising from or related to the application of the TFF Statutes or regulations, and not to take any dispute to any other judicial authorities;
   h. to report to TFF in writing any amendment made to its statutes and regulations as well as the list of its officials or persons who are authorised signatories with the right to sign legally binding agreements with third parties in 3 (three) weeks from the amendment;
   i. not to build any relations of a sporting nature with any entity that is not recognised by TFF or with any member whose membership has been suspended or terminated;
   j. to observe the principles of loyalty, integrity and good sporting behaviour through a statutory provision;
   k. to comply with the mandatory provisions specified under this Statute during its membership;
   l. to maintain a register of members which must be regularly updated;
   m. to comply fully with all other obligations arising from the Statutes and other regulations of FIFA (e.g., the FIFA Code of Ethics), UEFA or the TFF. Violation of the above-mentioned obligations by any Member may lead to sanctions provided in this Statute.

Article 14 Suspension

1. The Congress is responsible for suspending a Member. The Executive Committee may, however, suspend a Member that seriously and repeatedly violates its obligations as a Member with immediate effect. The suspension shall last until the next Congress, unless the Executive Committee has lifted it in the meantime.
2. A suspension must be confirmed at the Congress. If it is not confirmed, the suspension is automatically lifted.
3. A suspended Member shall lose its membership rights (including the right to vote). Other Members cannot entertain any sporting relation with a suspended Member. The Disciplinary Committee may impose further sanctions.
4. Members which do not participate in the sports activities or events organized by TFF for three (3) consecutive years shall be suspended from voting at the Congress until they have fulfilled their obligations in this respect and may not be candidate for any function with TFF.

Article 15 Expulsion

1. The Congress may expel a Member:
    a. if it fails to fulfill its financial obligations towards TFF; or
    b. if it seriously violates the Statutes, regulations, directives and decisions of FIFA, UEFA or TFF and has been sanctioned therefore.
2. For an expulsion to be valid, such expulsion must be approved by the Congress. The member in question shall have the right to speak in its own defense before the polling.

Article 16 Resignation

1. Any member may resign from the membership of TFF at the end of the playing season. Written notice of resignation must reach the General Secretariat of TFF before the second half of the beginning of that playing season.
2. The resignation shall not be valid until the Member wishing to resign has fulfilled its financial obligations towards TFF and other TFF Members.

Article 17 Results of promotion and relegation of TFF members

1. An amateur club duly registered with TFF and promoted to a professional league, automatically becomes a member of TFF. An amateur club promoted to a professional league must provide the General Secretariat with all documents enumerated in article 11 paragraphs 2 when applying for TFF membership. TFF Executive Committee decides the compatibility of the mentioned documents.

2. A club relegated from a professional league to an amateur league shall not lose its membership to TFF. However, as long as this club belongs to an amateur league, it has no right to be represented at the Congress and therefore loses those rights, which are related to the Congress. This club in question will be represented at the Congress by the Turkish Amateur Sports Clubs Confederation.

Article 18 Status of Clubs and TFF affiliated Unions

1. Clubs or any other unions affiliated to TFF shall be subordinated to and recognized by TFF.
   The statutes and regulations of these members or unions must be approved by the Executive Committee of TFF.
2. The Clubs and TFF affiliated unions shall take all their decisions on any matters regarding their membership independently of any institution or organization. This obligation applies regardless of their organizational structure.
3. No natural or legal person (including the holding companies and the subsidiaries) may administer or control more than one club or group in a way that would jeopardize the integrity of any match or competition.

III HONORARY PRESIDENT

Article 19 Honorary President

1. The Congress may bestow the title of Honorary President upon any person who served as President of the TFF and provided meritorious service to the game of football.
2. Nominate of Honorary President shall be designated by The Executive Committee.
3. The Honorary President may take part in the Congress and has the right to vote.

IV ORGANISATION

Article 20 Bodies of TFF

1. The organisation of TFF shall consist of the following bodies:
   a. Congress;
   b. President;
   c. Executive Committee;
   d. Emergency Committee;
   e. (Amended by the decision of Congress at 12.6.2009) Legal Committees;
   f. Auditing Committee;

  g. General Secretary.
2. TFF shall also consist of the following bodies with a consultative and/or administrative role:
   a. General Secretariat;
   b. Standing and ad-hoc committees.

A CONGRESS

Article 21 Definition and composition of Congress

1. (Amended by the decision of Congress at 29.06.2011) The Congress is the supreme decision-making organ of TFF
2. Only a Congress that is duly convoked has the authority to take decisions.
3. The Congress may be either an ordinary or an extraordinary Congress.
4. TFF shall conduct the proceedings regarding the Congress in compliance with the Standing orders of the Congress.
5. The Presiding Board shall conduct the proceedings regarding the Congress in compliance with the Standing orders of the Congress.
6. The Executive Committee may invite guests to Congress without the right to vote.
7. The Executive Committee and the General Secretary shall take part in the Congress without the right to vote.

Article 22 Delegates and votes

1. The Congress is composed of its following members represented by delegate(s) at the date of the call for a Congress meeting:
   a. The President of all the football clubs in the top Turkish Professional Football League and six delegates from each of them;
   b. The President of all the football clubs in Turkish Professional Football League 1 and one delegate from each of them;
   c. The President of all the football clubs in Turkish Professional Football League 2;
   d. The President of all the football clubs in Turkish Professional Football League 3;
   e. The Turkish Amateur Sports Clubs Confederation's President and nine delegates appointed by the Executive Committee of the Confederation;
   f. (Amended by the decision of Congress at 29.0.2011) The President of the Professional Footballers' Association and five delegates who are retired from professional football (These five delegates shall be appointed from among footballers who were capped most in Turkey's A National Team);
   g. (Amended by the decision of Congress at 29.06.2011) The President and five delegates of the Turkish Football Trainers Association (These five

delegates shall be appointed from among trainers who were served most as the head coach of Turkey's A National Team);

h. (Amended by the decision of Congress at 29.06.2011) The President and five delegates of the Active Football Referees and Observers Association. (These five delegates must be appointed from among retired referees who officiated most in UEFA Champions League except for the relegation matches, or the equal structured organisations before the establishment of the said league. The President and the said five delegates must be retired.);
i. The president of the disabled sports associations involved in football;
j. Each individual who served on the Executive Committee of FIFA or UEFA;
k. Each individual who served actively on the committees of FIFA or UEFA for a period of at least 10 years;
l. (Amended by the decision of Congress at 01.06.2019) Individuals who served as President of the Turkish Football Federation.

2. (Amended by the decision of Congress at 29.06.2011) Delegates, who represents the legal person natured members of TFF, must be appointed or elected by the appropriate body of that Member. They must provide evidence of proxy to the Congress upon request.
3. Each delegate has only one vote. Only the delegates present are entitled to vote. Voting by proxy or by letter is not permitted.
4. During their terms of office, the members of the Executive Committee and the General Secretary of TFF may not be appointed as delegates of the Congress.
5. Any individual who is employed by TFF, either on a salary or contract basis, or is paid an attendance allowance, shall not be eligible for election as a delegate to the Congress. Any such individual shall be eligible for election as a delegate to the Congress only if he/she has resigned from his/her office at least one year prior to the ordinary or extraordinary Congress meeting at which he/she wishes to be elected as a delegate.
6. A delegate must be a citizen of the Republic of Turkey.

Article 23 Authority of Congress

1. The Congress has the following authorities:
   a. to adopt and amend the Statutes of the TFF and the standing orders of the Congress,
   b. to elect the president, vice-president and two members of the Presiding Board of the Congress,
   c. to elect the President and full and substitute members of both the Executive Committee and the Auditing Committee,
   d. to approve the financial statements,
   e. to approve the budget,
   f. to approve the annual report of the Executive Committee,
   g. to empower the Executive Committee to amend the budget as and when needed,

h. to discharge the President and the Executive Committee,
i. to approve the annual audit reports drawn up by the Auditing Committee,
j. to empower the Executive Committee to purchase and sell real properties and to create rights-in-kind thereon,
k. to set up commissions during the congress, if needed,
l. to decide whether or not to bestow the title of Honorary President,
m. to admit, suspend or expel a member,
n. to approve all non-budgetary expenditures of the TFF,
o. to fulfil the duties assigned to itself under the related Law,
p. to fix the membership dues,
q. to approve the resignation of a member,
r. to revoke the mandate of a member of the TFF organs and member of TFF bodies appointed by itself,
s. to assess the requests of members in accordance with these Statutes.

2. Elections for the President, Executive Committee and other organs/bodies of the TFF may be renewed at any ordinary or extraordinary Congress.

Article 24 Quorum of Congress

1. Decisions passed by the Congress shall only be valid if the absolute majority of the members who are entitled to vote are duly represented.
2. If this quorum is not achieved, a second Congress shall take place 24 hours after the first with at least one third of all delegates present with the same agenda at the same place.
3. If this quorum is not achieved, a third Congress shall take place seven (7) days after the second, at the same time, with the same agenda at the same place, without majority.

Article 25 Decisions of the Congress

1. (Amended by the decision of Congress on 01.06.2019) Unless otherwise stipulated in this Statutes, decisions are taken by the simple majority of the votes. Spoiled or blank voting slips or any other forms of abstentions are disregarded in calculating the votes.
2. Any amendment of the TFF Statutes, the Standing Orders of the Congress and the admission, suspension and expulsion of a member shall require the support of at least two third of the total number of valid votes.
3. A decision that requires a vote shall be reached by a show of hands or by means of an electronic count. If a show of hands does not result in a clear majority in favour of a motion, the vote shall be taken by calling the roll in alphabetical order.
4. The delegates may ask for a secret ballot by simple majority.

5. (Added by the decision of Congress at 12.6.2009) An action for rescission can be filed against any decision taken at the TFF Congress in violation of the national law or the TFF Statute before the Court of First Instance, where the TFF has its Head-office, within 30 days from the relevant meeting date. The petty sessions procedure shall apply to such cases.

Article 26 Elections

1. Elections shall be conducted by secret ballot and must be free.
2. Election for President shall take place prior to the elections for the Executive Committee and the Auditing Committee.
3. The person who polls the majority of the eligible votes is elected. If the event of a tie, the election shall be renewed.
4. The votes shall be counted in public by the Presiding Board.
5. All those TFF organs/bodies which are duly elected by the Congress shall have a four (4) years mandate which is limited to that of the Executive Committee in any case.
6. If an Ordinary or Extraordinary Congress elects a new member of a TFF organ/ body during this period, his/her mandate only covers the remaining term of office.
7. Any mandate of a member elected at the Congress shall immediately start after the closing of the Congress where his/her election took place and shall end with the closing of the next elective Congress to be held in the 4th year of term of office. Any election during the term of office only covers the remaining period of the ordinary term of office of four years.

Article 27 Ordinary Congress

1. The Ordinary Congress shall convene on or before 31 July every year while the electoral Congress shall take place every four years within forty-five days following the date, on which the football leagues are registered, at such place and on such date as may be fixed by the Executive Committee.
2. (Amended by the decision of Congress on 01.06.2019) The agenda, date and place of the Ordinary Congress shall be fixed by the Executive Committee and announced in a nationally circulated daily newspaper and on the official web site of TFF (www.tff.org) and shall also be notified by TFF in writing to all the delegates in advance.
3. The written notice shall contain the agenda items, the financial statements, the independent auditors' reports and other relevant documents.

Annex II

Article 28 Ordinary Congress Agenda

1. The agenda of the Ordinary Congress shall be drawn up by the Executive Committee of TFF.
2. The Presiding President of the Ordinary Congress shall announce to the Congress the agenda items as stated in the notice of meeting.
3. The Congress shall not make a decision on any point not included in the agenda.
4. It is possible which do not contravene with the Statutes of the TFF. A written motion by at least one-fifth of the total number of the delegates is mandatory to add newly matters to agenda or change the current matters of the agenda. The motion shall be put to vote, which shall be by show of hands, and, if adopted by an absolute majority of the delegates present, it shall be included in the agenda. Such agenda matters shall be discussed after all the previously announced agenda items have been discussed and decided. However, no motion for election may be included in the agenda.

Article 29 Extraordinary Congress

1. The Executive Committee may convene an Extraordinary Congress at any time.
2. The Executive Committee shall convene an Extraordinary Congress in 30 days the latest if forty percent of the total number of the delegates makes such a request in writing through a notary public. The delegates making the request must be the duly authorised representatives of the members which they are representing. If an Extraordinary Congress is not convened by the Executive Committee within this deadline, the delegates who requested it may apply to FIFA.
3. (Amended by the decision of Congress on 01.06.2019) The agenda, date and place of the Extraordinary Congress shall be announced by the Executive Committee in a nationally circulated daily newspaper and on the official web site of TFF (www.tff.org) and shall also be notified by TFF in writing to all the delegates in advance.
4. When an Extraordinary Congress is convened upon the request of the delegates, the agenda must contain the points raised by those delegates.
5. If the agenda of an Extraordinary Congress includes a motion to hold elections, such motion shall require an affirmative vote of at least one more than half of the total number of the delegates. If so adopted, an electoral Extraordinary Congress shall take place within 30 days.
6. The new President, Executive Committee and Internal Audit Committee elected at that electoral Extraordinary Congress shall hold office until the next electoral Ordinary Congress.
7. The agenda of an Extraordinary Congress may not be altered.

Article 30 Amendments to Statutes and Standing Orders of Congress

1. Any proposals for an amendment to the Statutes must be submitted by a Member in writing with a brief explanation to the General Secretariat and have to be supported by at least four (4) other Members.
2. Any proposal to amend the standing orders of the Congress must be submitted by a Member in writing with a brief explanation to the General Secretariat.
3. (Added by the decision of Congress at 12.6.2009) An amendment duly made to the TFF's Statute or the Standing Orders of the Congress shall take effect on the date it is published in the Official Gazette.

Article 31 Minutes

1. The Presiding Board shall be responsible for recording the minutes at the Congress.
2. The minutes shall be signed by the Presiding President and other members of the Presiding Board at the end of the meeting.
3. The minutes shall be provided to the General Secretariat of TFF within seven (7) days after the closing of the Congress involved.

Article 32 Effective dates of decisions

Decisions passed by the Congress shall come into effect immediately after the closing of the Congress unless the Congress decides otherwise.

B EXECUTIVE COMMITTEE

Article 33 Composition of the Executive Committee

1. The Executive Committee shall consist of the President of TFF and fourteen members who shall be elected by the Congress.
2. At its first meeting during the term of office, the Executive Committee shall elect the first and second Vice-President from among its members for the period of its term of office. If the seat of the First or Second Vice-President becomes vacant, a replacement shall be elected within one month.
3. The fourteen full members and fourteen substitute members of the Executive Committee shall be elected by a majority vote of the Congress. It is not necessary for a member of the Executive Committee to be a Congress delegate.
4. In case of vacancy due to any reason within the Executive Committee, the Executive Committee elects the replacement out of the duly elected substitutes for the remaining term of office.
5. To be eligible as member of the Executive Committee, an individual must (cumulatively):
    a. be a Turkish citizen and at the age of at least 25;

b. not been suspended due to a violation of the TFF statutes or regulations for entire one year or a total of two years for various violations within the last five (5) years prior to the relevant election;
c. not have any financial overdue or debts out of tax or social security obligations;
d. have not been imprisoned for a term of more than two (2) years for any crime committed intentionally or convicted of any crime against the security of the State, the Constitutional order or the operation of that order, the national defense or State secrets, or of espionage, embezzlement, malversation, corruption, theft, fraud, forgery, breach of trust, fraudulent bankruptcy, conspiracy in public tenders, fraudulent breach of contractual obligations, laundering of illegally obtained assets, or smuggling, regardless of whether any time limit provided for in Article 53 of the Turkish Penal Code has elapsed;
e. any individual, who was convicted of any one of the moral turpitude crimes listed above, shall not be eligible for to be a member of the Executive Committee even if his/her punishment has been suspended, turned into a fine or pardoned;
f. (Amended by the decision of Congress at 29.06.2011) Declare in writing that he/she shall resign from any function such as president or board member of a TFF Member Club, which competes at the professional leagues immediately after his/her election.

6. All Executive Committee members may be re-elected.
7. Members of the Executive Committee may not at the same time be a member of any other TFF organs or TFF body, Presiding Board or Congress delegate.
8. In cases where the Congress is to convene in less than six months, no election shall be held to fill any vacancy on the Executive Committee. 4

Article 34 Meetings of Executive Committee

1. The Executive Committee shall meet at least once a month.
2. The invitations of the Executive Committee meetings shall be made by the President. If five (5) of the members request a meeting, the President must convene it within at least 20 days.
3. The President shall compile the agenda. Each member of the Executive Committee is entitled to propose items for inclusion in the agenda.
4. The General Secretary shall take part in the meetings of the Executive Committee in a consultative role.
5. A member absent from three consecutive Executive Committee meetings or from five consecutive Executive Committee meetings in total in a year without an excuse shall be discharged. Reasons for not attending an Executive Committee meeting shall be submitted in writing to the President prior to the meeting. The Executive Committee shall decide whether such reason for absence is acceptable or not.
6. The meetings of the Executive Committee shall not be held in public. The Executive Committee may, however, invite third parties to attend. Those third

parties shall not have the right to vote and may only express an opinion with the permission of the Executive Committee.

Article 35 Powers of the Executive Committee

1. The Executive Committee has the following powers:
   a. to register and to certify football teams, to categorise them into leagues and groups, to give names to leagues, to organise leagues, and to draw up the competition regulations including the provisions for promotion and relegation to be applicable,
   b. to register the results of matches, to postpone matches, to change the date, time and place of matches, to decide on matches not completed, matches disputed or matches the outcome of which have been influenced externally,
   c. to provide training to, and to take all steps necessary to help improve the professional skills of, managers, trainers, technical staff members, referees, players, healthcare staff members and others involved in the game of football, to provide them with all social security rights they are entitled to, to lay down the rules and regulations regarding their transfers between clubs and their activities, to fix the registration, to fix the license and transfer fees and levies to be collected from football-related activities, to offer certain levels of discounts to those, who prove their membership of grassroots unions through a letter of reference, on such fees and levies and to regulate such discounts,
   d. to decide exclusively the rules regarding the distribution of revenues generated from the royalty rights of the Turkish football leagues. However, while deciding these rules, it is compulsory that a certain portion of such royalty revenues are distributed to clubs competing in minor leagues,
   e. to decide applications filed by clubs for permission to establish football teams, and to supervise all related activities and undertakings,
   f. to award football clubs, players, club officials, coaches and trainers,
   g. according to the budgets approved by the Congress to set salaries, fees and fringe benefits of a maximum of two members of the TFF's Emergency Committee, and of the administrative staff in the TFF's Headquarters, regional offices and offices abroad, as well as the attendance allowances, compensations and travel and accommodation expenses entitlement of the TFF's other committees,
   h. to build or to make third parties build stadiums, training and healthcare facilities upon the approval of the Congress,
   i. to rent, operate, or to make third parties operate, facilities necessary for TFF's activities and business, and to provide all football-related equipment, materials and other similar supplies,
   j. to set up and to organise the TFF's offices both in Turkey and abroad,
   k. to adopt and to implement all regulations falling within its powers and for any football activity,

l. to draw up regulations and programmes regarding the broadcasting of football matches by television, radio, the Internet and all other similar sound and data carriers, and to issue exclusively special regulations on and supervise the exercise of the TFF's commercial and financial rights regarding football-related printed materials and commercials,
m. to appoint the president and members of Standing committees as proposed by the President,
n. to approve new standing committees or ad-hoc committee proposed by the President and to appoint their President, Vice-President and members,
o. to decide the applications submitted by clubs, players, coaches, trainers, referees, match officials and other parties involved in football which are not falling within the jurisdiction of the Dispute Resolution Committee or the Disciplinary Committees,
p. to prepare and convene the Ordinary and Extraordinary Congress of TFF,
q. to draw up TFF's budget,
r. approve decisions that have been made by the Referees' Committee and that might give rise to legal consequences and may be referred to the Arbitration Committee,
s. to exercise the powers granted to it by the Congress and perform the tasks assigned to it under the Law concerning TFF, the Statutes of TFF and other related laws,
t. to appoint the First and Second Vice-Presidents of the Executive Committee,
u. to ensure that all national and international regulations and laws of the game are applied,
v. to ensure that players provide the necessary samples for doping control at the accredited Doping Control Centre in Turkey, and to administer the decisions of the national and international committees regarding the players tested positive,
w. to authorise the President and a Vice-President to incur certain expenses exceeding the annual budget decided by the Executive Committee annually,
x. to take steps to prevent violence in sports and to work in coordination with the related authorities to that end,
y. to appoint or to dismiss the General Secretary on the proposal of the President,
z. Executive Committee may delegate its powers to some of its members by defining the boundaries of such powers when necessary. These members may convene, take decisions and administer these decisions when needed. It is mandatory for these decisions to be informed and approved by the next Executive Committee.
aa. (Amended by the decision of Congress on 01.06.2019) to appoint the president, full and substitute members of the Disciplinary Committee, Appeals Committee, Club Licensing Committee and Ethics Committee and Dispute Resolution Chamber on the proposal of the President,

bb. (Annulled by the decision of Congress at 29.06.2011)
2. The places of assignment of the administrative units shall be decided by the Executive Committee.
3. The Executive Committee shall draw up and carry out regulations as it may deem proper and necessary for performing the tasks assigned to it here-above.

Article 36 Decisions of the Executive Committee

1. (Amended by the decision of Congress on 01.06.2019) The Executive Committee shall not engage in valid debate unless the simple majority of its members are present.
2. (Amended by the decision of Congress on 01.06.2019) The Executive Committee shall take decisions by a simple majority of the members present. In the event of a tied vote, the President shall have the casting vote. Voting by proxy or by letter is not permitted.
3. Any member of the Executive Committee must abstain from the debate and from taking decision if there is a potential conflict of interest.
4. The decisions taken shall be recorded in the minutes.
5. The decisions taken by the Executive Committee shall come into effect immediately, unless the Executive Committee decides otherwise.

C PRESIDENT

Article 37 President

1. The President is the legal representative of the TFF.
2. The duties and powers of the President are:
   a. implementing the decisions passed by the Congress and the Executive Committee through the General secretariat,
   b. ensuring the effective functioning of the bodies of TFF in order that they achieve the objectives described in these Statutes,
   c. proposing the appointment and the dismissal of the General Secretary,
   d. executing the relationship between TFF and its Members, FIFA, UEFA, political bodies and other national or international organizations,
   e. carrying out the business of the TFF in accordance with the organizational regulations of TFF, the present Statutes and other related provisions,
   f. supervising the work of the General secretariat,
   g. proposing the formation of standing committees and the appointment of the president and members of such standing committees to the Executive Committee,
   h. making expenditures in the name of the TFF and delegating this power to the Vice-Presidents, the General Secretariat or other staff members, if necessary,

i. if necessary, taking part in and chairing the meetings of the standing committees,
j. (Amended by the decision of Congress on 01.06.2019) proposing individuals for election to the Executive Committee as President and members of both the Disciplinary Committee, Appeals Committee, Club Licensing Committee, Ethics Committee and Dispute Resolution Chamber,
k. proposing individuals for election to the Executive Committee as President and full and substitute members of the Amateur and Professional Football Disciplinary Committees,
l. approving the Provincial Disciplinary Committees elected,
m. performing such other tasks as assigned to the President under the Statutes of TFF.

3. The President shall chair the Executive and Emergency Committee meetings and those committees of which he has been appointed president.
4. The President shall have the casting vote in the case of a tie at Executive Committee meetings.
5. (Amended by the decision of Congress at 29.06.2011) If the President is absent, the first Vice-President replaces him/her. If the first Vice-President is absent, the second Vice-President replaces him/her. If also the second Vice-President is absent the longest serving member of the Executive Committee replaces him/her.
6. In the cases of the President's death, resignation or permanently prevention of performing his/her functions, the first Vice-President shall represent him until the next Congress. This upcoming Congress shall elect a new President for the remaining term of office.

Article 38 Candidates for the office of the President

1. (Amended by the decision of Congress on 01.06.2019) A person wishing to be the candidate for the office of President at the Congress, must submit a written application to the TFF General Secretariat not later than seven (7) days prior to the date of the related Congress. All candidates for President applied in the mentioned time limit shall be announced on the official website of TFF (www.tff.org) beginning from six (6) days prior to the date of the related Congress.
2. Furthermore candidates for the office of President must present a letter of nomination signed by at least one-fifth of the delegates to the Presiding Board of the Congress. However, each delegate can only propose only one nominate.
3. To be eligible as TFF President, an individual must:
   a. be a Turkish citizen and at the age of at least 25,
   b. have not been suspended for a term of two years in total within the last five years prior to the relevant election,
   c. not have any overdue or debts out of tax or social security obligations,
   d. have not been imprisoned for a term of more than two (2) years for any crime committed intentionally or convicted of any crime against the

security of the State, the Constitutional order or the operation of that order, the national defense or State secrets, or of espionage, embezzlement, malversation, corruption, theft, fraud, forgery, breach of trust, fraudulent bankruptcy, conspiracy in public tenders, fraudulent breach of contractual obligations, laundering of illegally obtained assets, or smuggling, regardless of whether any time limit provided for in Article 53 of the Turkish Penal Code has elapsed.

e. Any individual, who was convicted of any one of the moral turpitude crimes listed above, shall not be eligible for the office of president even if his/her punishment has been suspended, turned into a fine or pardoned.
f. (Amended by the decision of Congress at 29.06.2011) To declare in writing that he/she shall resign from any function such as president or board member of a TFF Member Club which competes at TFF's professional leagues immediately after his/her election.

4. The election for the President shall take place before the election for the fourteen full and fourteen substitute members of the Executive Committee at the Congress.
5. The President shall be elected by majority vote of the delegates present at the Congress.
6. The President shall hold office for a term of four years.

Article 39 Representation and signature

1. The President is the legal representative of TFF and is entitled to sign on behalf of TFF.
2. The Executive Committee determines the Executive Committee Members and other officials who are entitled to sign on behalf of TFF in accordance with the provisions of these Statutes by taking into account of the organization of TFF.

D EMERGENCY COMMITTEE

Article 40 Emergency Committee

1. The Emergency Committee shall consist of the President of TFF, the Vice-Presidents and two Executive Committee members to be appointed by the President. The term of office of the Emergency Committee shall be limited to that of the Executive Committee.
2. The President shall convene the Emergency Committee meetings.
3. The Emergency Committee shall deal with all matters requiring immediate settlement between two meetings of the Executive Committee.
4. The General Secretary shall take part in the Emergency Committee's meetings. The Executive Committee may, if it deems necessary, invite consultants

and experts to attend any meeting of the Emergency Committee. However, no such consultant or expert shall have right to vote.

5. Decisions passed by the Emergency Committee meetings shall take effect immediately and be approved by the Executive Committee at its next meeting.
6. In the event that the President is unable to attend a meeting, the First Vice-President shall chair that meeting.

E AUDITING COMMITTEE

Article 41 Auditing Committee

1. The Auditing Committee shall consist of five full and five substitute members who must have expert knowledge in the field of finance and shall be elected by the Congress for an office term of four years. Members of the Auditing Committee shall be eligible for re-election. It is not necessary for an Auditing Committee member to be a delegate of the Congress.
2. The full members shall elect a President from among themselves.
3. The Auditing Committee shall audit the financial activities of the TFF in the name of the Congress in accordance with the regulations drawn up by the Executive Committee and approved by the Congress. The Auditing Committee shall prepare an annual audit report and submit it to the Congress for approval.
4. The Auditing Committee members may perform their duties either collectively or appoint one auditor from among themselves to conduct the necessary examinations and audit on certain subject matters and accordingly draw up an audit report which shall be signed by all the members of the Auditing Committee and presented as a joint report.
5. (Amended by the decision of Congress on 01.06.2019) Decisions at meetings of the Auditing Committee shall be adopted by majority vote of its members. A member dissenting from a decision shall provide the Congress a report stating the reasons for his dissenting vote.
6. An annual audit report shall contain income and expense statements, balance sheets and other financial statements regarding the TFF's annual activities. They shall also provide an opinion on whether the financial resources available have been used efficiently, cost effectively and productively, whether expenditures have been incurred in connection with the TFF's activities, and whether financial decisions and transactions have been carried out for their intended purposes and programmes.
7. (Amended by the decision of Congress at 29.06.2011) The Auditing Committee shall send its audit report to the Congress delegates at least fifteen days prior to the date of the Congress.

F STANDING COMMITTEES

Article 42 Standing Committees

1. The standing committees of the TFF are:
   a. Referees' Committee,
   b. (Amended by the decision of Congress at 12.6.2009) Committee of Delegates,
   c. Sports Medical Committee,
   d. International Relations Committee,
   e. Committee of Social Responsibility and Fair Play,
   f. Other Standing Committees.
2. The number of members, composition, procedures, of all Standing Committees are duly defined in the specific terms of references adopted by the Executive Committee taking into account the nature and characteristics of the service it shall provide.
3. Each president shall represent his own standing committee. The standing committees shall conduct business in compliance with the relevant organisation regulations drawn up by the Executive Committee.
4. Each president shall exercise the fixing of the dates of meetings, performing all tasks regarding its business and reporting back to the Executive Committee by means of the General Secretary.
5. All opinions, proposals and reports of these committees shall be of a consultative nature and shall not be put into effect unless approved by the President and the Executive Committee.
6. Each committee may propose amendments at any regulations to the Executive Committee regarding its working area.
7. The term of office of each standing committee shall be limited to that of the Executive Committee.

Article 43 (Amended by the decision of Congress at 12.6.2009) Referees' Committee

1. The Referees' Committee shall consist of one president and eight (8) members.
2. The members of the Referees' Committee must be appointed from among referees who retired at least one year before the date of their appointment to the Committee. Not more than 3 (three) members of the Committee, including the President, may be appointed from among individuals who has experience in the field of sports but who have not served as referee.
3. The Referees' Committee is fully independent at its decisions. No member of the Referees' Committee shall be replaced unless he has resigned or is deemed to have resigned duly.
4. The Referees' Committee shall be responsible for appointing the referees for any official or friendly matches within the authority of TFF to be played

between member clubs, for reviewing and deciding technical disputes arising from these matches in relation to the Laws of the Game according to the given competence by the IFAB Board, establishing local referees' committees in cities and districts, providing training to referees, categorizing referees, drawing up promotion and relegation regulations for referees and performing such other tasks as may be assigned to it under the present Statutes and other relevant regulations.

Article 44 (Amended by the decision of Congress at 12.6.2009) Committee of Delegates

1. The Committee of Delegates shall consist of one president and six (6) members who have vast, reliable knowledge and experience in sports.
2. This Committee is fully independent at its decisions. No member of this Committee shall be replaced unless he has resigned or is deemed to have resigned duly.
3. The Committee Delegates shall be responsible for assigning delegates for official and friendly matches, categorizing delegates, trains delegates in collaboration with the Football Development Center and performing such other tasks as may be assigned to it under relevant regulations.

Article 45 Sports Medical Committee

1. The Sports Medical Committee shall consist of members holding medical degree and take all necessary steps to protect the good health of players.
2. The Anti-doping Sub-committee is the subsidiary of the Sports Medical Committee.

Article 46 International Relations Committee

1. The International Relations Committee shall represent and promote Turkish football abroad and provide assistance in the improvement of the TFF's international relations.

Article 47 Committee of Fair Play and Social Responsibility

1. The Committee of Fair Play and Social Responsibility shall deal with everything related to the promotion of the rules of Fair Play and the principles of integrity and sportsmanship as well as the creation of social responsibility conscious.

Article 48 Ad-hoc Committees

1. The Executive Committee may, if necessary, create ad-hoc committees for special duties and for a limited period of time. The Executive Committee appoints its members and approves its terms of references.

G GENERAL SECRETARIAT

Article 49 General Secretariat and Administrative Units

1. The General secretariat is the administrative body and carry out all the administrative work of TFF under the responsibility of the General Secretary.
2. The General Secretariat consists of several administrative units regulated in the organisational regulations adopted by the Executive Committee.
3. The administrative units shall be responsible for ensuring that the services and activities of TFF are carried out in accordance with the TFF statutes, regulations and decision as well as directives by the competent bodies.
4. The members of the General secretariat fulfil their given tasks in the best manner and in line with the objectives set.

Article 50 General Secretary

1. The General Secretary is the chief executive of the General Secretariat and responsible against the Executive Committee.
2. The General Secretary shall be appointed by the Executive Committee upon the proposal of the President of the TFF.
3. The General Secretary shall be responsible for:
   a. carrying out decisions adopted by the Congress and Executive Committee in compliance with the President's directives,
   b. organising the Congress and meetings of the Executive Committee, the Emergency Committee and standing committees,
   c. attending, or, in his absence, appointing a proxy to attend, the Congress, the meetings of the Executive Committee, the Emergency Committee and the Standing committees as well as the ones of the ad-hoc committees without the right to vote,
   d. ensuring that the minutes for the meetings of the Executive Committee, Emergency Committee and the Standing committees are properly compiled,
   e. managing and keeping the accounts of the TFF properly,
   f. carrying out the correspondence of the TFF,
   g. handling relations with members, committees, FIFA and UEFA,
   h. proposing managerial staff to the Executive Committee for approval,
   i. organizing the structure of TFF according to the directives given by the Executive Committee.

4. The General Secretary may not be a Congress delegate or a member of any other statutory organ/body of TFF.

Article 51 Domestic Organisation of TFF

1. TFF forms its domestic organization by appointing voluntary football representatives in all cities or setting up regional TFF directorates or liaison offices, consisting of adequate number of employees, in such cities as may be decided by the Executive Committee.
2. These representatives shall perform the duties assigned to them by the TFF, report to TFF all material events and incidents that occur in their respective geographical areas of responsibility, and carry out such other tasks assigned to them to help improve football.

Article 52 TFF's Offices Abroad

1. The Executive Committee may decide to open TFF offices with adequate number of employees in such countries as it may deem fit and subject the prior approval of FIFA and the respective Association.

Article 53 Right of Disposal

1. TFF shall be entitled to acquire or otherwise, purchase, sell, rent, lease let and manage such movable and immovable assets, which it may deem necessary for or conducive to attaining its objectives, or create liens or any other types of limited rights-in-kind on any such asset in accordance with its budgetary guidelines and these Statutes.
2. TFF shall also be entitled to accept donations and establish or invest in economic enterprises and companies of any kind.

H LEGAL COMMITTEES

Article 54 (Amended by the decision of Congress at 12.6.2009) Legal Committees

1. The TFF's Legal Committees shall be as follows:
    a. Dispute Resolution Committee;
    b. Disciplinary Committees;
    c. Club Licensing Committee;
    d. Ethics Committee; and
    e. Arbitration Committee.

2. The rules and procedures governing the work of each of these Committees shall be stipulated by the Club Licensing Regulations, Football Disciplinary Regulations, Arbitration Committee Regulations, Dispute Resolution Committee Regulations and other related regulations.
3. Any decision made by any one of the TFF's Legal Committees shall be final and binding and shall have the same effect as a conclusive verdict in respect of the parties involved, if not appealed against before the Arbitration Committee within seven days following the receipt of notice of the decision and/or following the promulgation of any relevant regulations or directives. Appealing against any such decision before any court of law is strictly prohibited.
4. A member of any Legal Committee shall not at the same time work for any affiliated member or club of the TFF or have a seat on the Executive Board, any other Standing or ad-hoc Committee or in the General Secretariat. Any such member must act fully independently and impartially at all times in executing his/her duties pursuant to his/her mandate.

Article 55 (Amended by the decision of Congress on 01.06.2019) Dispute Resolution Committee

1. The Dispute Resolution Committee shall consist of a President, a Vice-President and six full members and six substitute members who shall be appointed by the Executive Committee upon the proposal of the President of the TFF who must have at least five years of professional experience in the area of law.
2. The term of office the Dispute Resolution Committee shall be limited to that of the TFF Executive Committee. The Dispute Resolution Committee shall elect a vice-president and a rapporteur from among its members.
3. No individual serving at the TFF's Executive Committee, Auditing Committee and other chamber or committee or actively in charge at sports club including appointed or elected duties, professional football players, coaches, medical team, match agents and intermediaries cannot be a member of Dispute Resolution Committee.
4. The Dispute Resolution Committee is fully independent in its decisions.
   No member of the Dispute Resolution Committee shall be replaced unless he/she has resigned or is duly deemed to have resigned from office. When any vacancies occur on the Dispute Resolution Committee for any reason, the substitute members shall fill such vacancies in the order of their appointment and hold office for the remaining balance of the term of office.
5. At least five members must be present in order to take valid decisions. Decisions are passed with the support of at least the simple majority of the members present. In the event of a tied vote, the President shall have the casting vote.

Annex II

Article 56 (Amended by the decision of Congress on 01.06.2019) Duties and Powers of the Dispute Resolution Committee

1. If the parties accept the jurisdiction of the Dispute Resolution Chamber, it shall have the jurisdiction over the disputes born between Clubs, players, trainers, players agents, arising out of contracts regarding football. The disputes regarding training compensation and sporting sanctions must be resolved by Dispute Resolution Chamber exclusively.
2. If either of the parties who is represented by an attorney at law, the Committee, shall decide for a fix attorney fee defined at the official fee tariff for the civil courts of law.
3. The working principles and procedure of Dispute Resolution Chamber shall be enacted by the Executive Committee by a Regulation.

Article 57 Disciplinary Committees

1. Disciplinary Committees shall consist of bodies at three different levels:
    a. The provincial disciplinary committees;
    b. the Amateur Football Disciplinary Committee;
    c. the Professional Football Disciplinary Committee.
2. Members of the Amateur Football Disciplinary Committee and the Professional Football Disciplinary Committee shall be appointed by the Executive Committee upon the proposal of the President of the TFF and, while members of provincial disciplinary committees shall be appointed by the President of the TFF.
3. (Amended by the decision of Congress at 29.06.2011) The Amateur Football Disciplinary Committee and the Professional Football Disciplinary Committee shall each consist of one president and six members, while a provincial disciplinary committee shall have one president and two to four members, depending on the extent of the sports activities actively carried out in the related city. Substitute members to be appointed shall be equivalent to full members in number.
4. The term of office of each disciplinary committee shall be limited to that of the Executive Committee.
5. (Amended by the decision of Congress at 01.06.2019) Any full and substitute members to be elected to these disciplinary committees must hold a bachelor's or an associate degree. Any person who will serve as president, vice-president or rapporteur must hold a bachelor's degree in law. The members of the both Professional and Amateur Football Disciplinary Committee must have at least five years of professional experience in the area of law.
6. The principles and procedures regarding the disciplinary committees shall be governed by the Regulations approved by the Executive Committee.
7. The powers of the Congress and the Executive Committee with regard to the suspension and expulsion of Members are reserved.

Article 58 Disciplinary Measures

1. All disciplinary infringements and unsportsmanlike behaviors committed by clubs and individuals during football matches and organizations and the disciplinary measures that shall be imposed on such clubs and individuals shall be regulated at the TFF Disciplinary regulations approved by the TFF Executive Committee in accordance with generally accepted national and international practices and the disciplinary regulations of FIFA and UEFA.
2. Disciplinary Committees shall review and decide on all disciplinary infringements and unsportsmanlike behaviors committed by clubs or individuals.
3. The disciplinary measures that shall be imposed for such disciplinary infringements and unsportsmanlike behaviors are primarily:
   1. for real and legal persons:
      a. a warning;
      b. a reprimand;
      c. a fine;
      d. the return of awards.
   2. for real persons:
      a. a warning;
      b. an expulsion;
      c. a match suspension;
      d. a ban from the dressing rooms and/or the substitutes' bench;
      e. a ban from entering a stadium;
      f. a ban on taking part in any football-related activity;
      g. suspension of license.
   3. for legal persons:
      a. a transfer ban;
      b. playing a match without spectators;
      c. playing a match on neutral territory;
      d. a ban on playing in a particular stadium;
      e. a ban on accepting spectators to a particular stand or a portion thereof;
      f. annulment of the result of the match;
      g. expulsion;
      h. a defeat by forfeit;
      i. deduction of points;
      j. relegation to a lower league.

Article 59 Club Licensing Committee

1. (Amended by the decision of Congress at 29.06.2011) The Club Licensing Committee shall decide on whether a licence should be granted to an applicant club or taken back or whether to apply sanctions on the basis of the documents provided and in accordance with the TFF club licensing regulations.
2. When evaluating a club, the Club Licensing Committee shall base its evaluations on the sporting criteria, infrastructure criteria, administrative criteria, legal criteria, financial criteria, and personnel criteria.

3. (Amended by the decision of Congress at 01.06.2019) The Club Licensing Committee shall consist of a President, a Vice-President and seven (7) full members and seven (7) substitute members who shall be appointed by the Executive Committee upon the proposal of the President of the TFF. The members of the Committee shall be selected as follows;
    a) One member shall be a lawyer who has minimum experience of 5 years in the area of law.
    b) One member shall be a Sworn in Certified Public Accountant who is authorized as it is described under Law of Accounting Profession.
    c) Two members shall be an independent auditor as described under 660 no Decree Law (Executive Order) Public Oversight Accounting and Auditing Standards Authority
    d) One member shall be a Certified Public Accountant who is authorized as it is described under Law of Accounting Profession
    e) Two members shall be graduated from a university degree of business administration or finance with a minimum five years of experience in the field.
4. The term of office of the Club Licensing Committee is four (4) years and in any case limited to the term of office of the Executive Committee of TFF.
5. No member of the Club Licensing Committee shall be replaced unless he has resigned or is deemed to have resigned duly.
6. (Amended by the decision of Congress at 01.06.2019) At least five members must be present in order to make valid meeting. Decisions shall be passed with the support of the simple majority of the members present.
7. The members of the Club Licensing Committee shall neither be a Delegate of the Congress nor belong to any other TFF organ or body at the same time. The members of the Club Licensing Committee may be re-elected.
8. The principles and the proceeding of the Club Licensing Committee shall be governed by the club licensing regulations approved by the TFF Executive Committee.

Article 60 Ethics Committee

1. The Committee of Ethics shall consist of a president and four (4) full and four (4) substitute members who shall be elected by the Executive Committee on the proposal of the President of TFF. Each member of the Committee of Ethics must hold a bachelor's degree in law and have a minimum of 5 years of professional experience in the field of law. The Committee of Ethics shall be responsible for preserving the ethical values and the brand value of Turkish football and carrying out all necessary legal inspections to prevent any damage to football's good reputation in society.
2. The term of office of the Committee of Ethics shall be four (4) years and shall in any case be limited to that of the Executive Committee of TFF.
3. No member of the Committee of Ethics shall be replaced unless he has resigned or is deemed to have resigned duly.

4. At least three members must be present in order for the Committee of Ethics to make valid meeting. Decisions shall be passed with the support of the simple majority of the members present
5. The members of the Committee of Ethics shall neither be a delegate of the Congress nor serve on any other TFF organ or body at the same time. The members of the Committee of Ethics shall be eligible for re-election.
6. The principles and the proceeding of the Committee of Ethics shall be governed by the Committee of Ethics regulations approved by the TFF Executive Committee.

Article 61 Arbitration Committee

1. The Arbitration Committee shall consist of a President, a Vice-President and six full members and six substitute members who shall be appointed by the Executive Committee upon the proposal of the President of the TFF who must have at least five years of professional experience in the area of law. The related regulations of FIFA and UEFA are predicated on appointing the members.
2. The term of office of the Board of Arbitration is limited to the term of office of the Executive Committee of TFF. The Board of Arbitration shall elect a vice-president and a rapporteur from among its members.
3. (Amended by the decision of Congress at 01.06.2019) Until they resign no individual serving on any committee of a self-governing association or a sports club, or suspended by any sanctions or disciplinary committee for a term of more than six months shall not be eligible for election as a member of the Board of Arbitration.
4. The Arbitration Committee is fully independent when conducting its functions. No member of the Arbitration Committee shall be replaced unless he/she has resigned or is duly deemed to have resigned from office. When any vacancies occur on the Arbitration Committee for any reason, the substitute members shall fill such vacancies in the order of their appointment and hold office for the remaining balance of the term of office.
5. At least five members must be present in order to take valid decisions. Decisions are passed with the support of at least the simple majority of the members present. In the event of a tied vote, the President shall have the casting vote.
6. The Arbitration Committee may call for opinions, information and documents from any related party and compile any relevant evidence with regard to matters referred to the Arbitration Committee. It may also summon and hear any relevant party.
7. The Arbitration Committee shall conduct all proceedings in accordance with these Statutes and the regulations of FIFA and UEFA and by taking into consideration of the related provisions of laws concerning such proceedings and after due consideration, admit or dismiss a complaint or decide that an administrative decision appealed be amended, whether in part or in whole.

8. Awards rendered by the Arbitration Committee shall be enforced by the General Secretary and the President.
9. The rules of procedure for the Board of Arbitration shall be specified by regulations drawn up by the Executive Committee.

Article 62 Duties and Powers of the Arbitration Committee

1. The Arbitration Committee shall review and make its final decision on the disputes listed below upon the request of the relevant parties:
   a. resolutions adopted by the Executive Committee in relation to disputes that arose between TFF and clubs, referees, players, coaches, trainers, players' agents, healthcare staff members and other officials,
   b. (Amended by the decision of Congress on 29.06.2011) decisions awarded by the Amateur and Professional Football Disciplinary Committees,
   c. decisions awarded by the Dispute Resolution Committee,
   d. decisions awarded by the Club Licensing Committee,
   e. decisions awarded by the Ethics Committee,
   f. decisions which have legal effects awarded by the other bodies of TFF that are authorised under the TFF's Statutes and regulations to make final decisions, and
   g. regulations issued by the Executive Committee.
2. Any party directly affected by the above-mentioned resolution or regulation, may appeal against it in written form before the Arbitration Committee within seven days after the date of the receipt of that resolution or the publication of that regulation.
3. Decisions of the Arbitration Committee shall be final and binding. Decisions of the Arbitration Committee shall not be subject to the approval of any administrative or judicial authority and it is prohibited to take any decision awarded by the Arbitration Committee before any administrative or judicial authority.

Article 63 (Amended by the decision of Congress at 12.6.2009) Jurisdiction of Legal Committees

1. (Amended by the decision of Congress at 29.06.2011) The TFF, its members, clubs, referees, players, coaches, trainers, player's agents, match agents, healthcare staff members and other officials may not take any football-related dispute to any other judicial authorities other than the Legal Committees, unless specifically stipulated otherwise in the present Statute and the regulations of both FIFA and UEFA.
2. Any dispute in relation to above-said jurisdiction shall be resolved by the Legal Committees of FIFA, UEFA or the TFF.
3. The TFF shall have jurisdiction over internal disputes and FIFA over international disputes.

Article 64 Court of Arbitration for Sport (CAS/TAS)

1. In accordance with the FIFA and UEFA Statutes, any appeal against a final and binding FIFA or UEFA decision shall be heard by the Court of Arbitration for Sport (CAS) in Lausanne, Switzerland. CAS shall not, however, hear appeals on violations of the Laws of the Game, suspensions according to relevant provisions of the FIFA and UEFA Statutes or decisions passed by the independent and duly constituted Arbitration Committee of TFF.
2. TFF shall ensure its full compliance and that of its Members, Players, Officials and match and players' agents with any final decision passed by a FIFA or UEFA body as well as CAS.

V FINANCE

Article 65 Financial period and budget of TFF

1. The financial period of the TFF shall begin on 1 June and end on 31 May every year.
2. The budget of the TFF shall be prepared by the Executive Committee depending on the financial period involved and submitted to the Congress and shall be effective after approval.
3. Revenues, expenses and activities of the TFF, the funds to be allocated to such activities, staff remunerations, expenses of committees and other overhead costs shall be specified in the budget on a balance sheet basis and in accordance with the budgetary basis drawn up by the Executive Committee.
4. The President of the TFF shall be entitled to perform such cash collections and incur such expenses as described in the Law concerning the TFF and the present Statute in accordance with the related budgetary rules.
5. The TFF shall set aside reserve funds in order to guarantee its prime future operations.

Article 66 Revenues

1. The revenue of the TFF arises from:
   a. (Amended by the decision of Congress at 12.6.2009) 15% royalty collected from clubs in relation to football betting games and fixed-odds betting games.
   b. 10% of the proceeds received by clubs from matches broadcast on TV, radio, the Internet or via any other similar data carrier and from any contract they have signed with any media company. However, this rate shall be 1% in the case of proceeds generated from a contract regarding the broadcasting of a friendly match or preparatory match;
   c. sponsorship revenues;

d. net proceeds from official and friendly National Team matches, remaining after all legally required deductions, as well as those proceeds derived from such matches broadcast on TV, radio, the Internet or via any other similar data carrier;
e. registration and registration renewal fees, transfer levies, subscriptions, etc.;
f. proceeds derived from the TFF's fixed assets and from other activities such as the transfer, assignment, sale and lease of its real properties;
g. Income from all kinds of economic enterprises and corporations, whether established or invested in by the TFF;
h. Interest receipts;
i. Donations and grants; and
j. Others.

Article 67 Expenditures

1. With a view to fulfilling its responsibilities, the TFF shall be entitled to incur any and all expenses in accordance with the Law concerning the TFF and the TFF's budgetary basis.
2. In every budget year, the TFF distributes 15% of its total annual revenue to second and third league member clubs for projects submitted by them to the TFF and approved by the Executive Committee until 1 April, and another 15% thereof to related committees, organizations, institutions and sports clubs for infrastructural, training, sports facility or football development projects which must be related to the game of football submitted by them to the TFF and approved by the Executive Committee until 1 April, in return for a contribution from such parties, provided only that such decisions are adopted in accordance with the TFF's regulations regarding resource utilization and approved by the Congress.
3. The TFF shall be entitled to determine the scope or nature of such projects beforehand.
4. Non-budgetary expenditures that the TFF may intend to incur shall be subject to the prior approval of the Congress.
5. (Amended by the decision of Congress at 01.06.2019) These expenditures include funds to be allocated under a protocol for training and sports facility projects in return for the right to use the sports facilities, which have been transferred or leased by the Ministry of Youth and Sports and or public authorities to, or on which time limited usufruct rights have been created to the benefit of, sports clubs or public authorities under a protocol, including the VIP stands thereat, and also to benefit from the services of the staff members of the General Directorate of Youth and Sports.

Article 68 (Amended by the decision of Congress at 12.6.2009) Independent Audit

1. The financial condition and profit/loss statements of the TFF shall be audited annually by an independent auditor that has audit experience in the international sports industry.
2. All audit reports shall be disclosed to the public after they are reviewed by the Congress.
3. A copy of the audit report shall be distributed to the Congress delegates prior to the date of the Congress in accordance with the related provisions of these Statutes.
4. An audit firm shall not provide audit services to the TFF for more than five consecutive years.

Article 69 Membership dues

1. The annual membership fee is due on 1 July.
2. The subscription fee for any new member shall be paid within thirty (30) days of the close of the Congress at which they are admitted.
3. The Congress shall fix the amount of the subscription fee on the proposal of the TFF Executive Committee. The subscription fee shall be same for every Member.

Article 70 (Amended by the decision of Congress at 12.6.2009) Compensation and the priority of the receivables of TFF

1. The TFF may debit any Member's account to settle claims.
2. A fine imposed by the TFF on a Member club in accordance with Article 15 of Law No. 5894 shall first be deducted from the sums due by the TFF to such Member club.

Article 71 Levies

1. Any TFF member may demand from its own members a levy to be paid for matches. Such levy is subject to the approval of the TFF Executive Committee.

VI COMPETITIONS AND RIGHTS IN COMPETITIONS AND EVENTS

Article 72 Competitions

1. TFF organizes and coordinates any official competition held within its territory. TFF organizes the following competitions:

a. Super League;
b. Championship of the 1st League, 2nd League and 3rd League;
c. Amateur League competitions;
d. National Cup competitions;
e. Youth competitions for different age groups;
f. Women's competitions;
g. Disabled competitions;
h. Futsal competitions;
i. Beach football competitions;
j. Regional competitions;
k. Veteran competitions.

2. TFF shall take into account the coordinated international calendar compiled by FIFA and the principle of promotion and relegation while organizing the competitions.
3. The Executive Committee may create new competitions and adopt for each competition the appropriate competition regulations.

Article 73 Intellectual and Industrial Property Rights

1. The TFF is the exclusive owner of all the brands, logos, including all the rights to use them, and all other similar intellectual and industrial property rights that the TFF is or will be using. The existence of these rights shall not prejudice the right of the TFF to have them registered with the Turkish Patent Institute and any International Patent Office in the name of the TFF.

Article 74 Authorization for Broadcasting

1. The Executive Committee of the TFF shall be exclusively entitled to grant the right to broadcast matches on television, radio, the Internet and all other similar sound and data carriers, and to organize and plan such broadcasts.
2. (Added by the decision of Congress at 12.6.2009) The above-said power encompasses particularly the marketing of the TFF's broadcasting rights centrally and the distribution of the proceeds derived from such rights to Member clubs in such manner as may be decided by the relevant bodies of the TFF.
3. When exercising the said power, the Executive Committee shall prioritize the interests of Turkish football, clubs and the TFF.
4. Encrypted broadcasting of national teams is prohibited.
5. Mobile rights shall be regulated exclusively by the Executive Committee of the TFF.
6. Any agreement signed between a club and a broadcasting company shall be subject to the TFF's supervision and approval. Any such agreement not approved by the TFF shall not be binding on the TFF. No match shall be broadcast on TV, radio, the Internet and all other similar sound and data carriers, unless the required license therefore has been received from the TFF.

7. (Amended by the decision of Congress at 01.06.2019) The rules and procedures governing the cooperation among the Ministry of Youth and Sports, the Provincial Directorates and Provincial Offices regarding the broadcasting of matches shall be laid down in a Protocol Regarding the Utilization of Sports Facilities and Services of Personnel.
8. The rules and procedures regarding the broadcasting of matches, and the rights that may be given to and the sanctions that may be imposed on broadcasting companies and clubs shall be specified in the Broadcasting Regulations to be drawn up by the Executive Committee.
9. The TFF shall be entitled to draw up specifications, hold tenders and sign agreements on behalf of clubs with regard to licenses for broadcasting league matches on TV and radio. The TFF may consult with the Clubs' Union regarding the broadcasting rights of the Super League.
10. The tender for broadcasting rights shall be held not earlier than one year and not later than six months prior to the expiry of the existing broadcasting license.

Article 75 Club Licensing System

1. The participation of a professional football club in the national and UEFA club competitions is subject to a licence granted by the competent TFF organs.
2. For TFF competitions, the licensing process, the competent bodies as well as the set of licensing criteria are described in the TFF Club Licensing Regulations issued by the Executive Committee.
3. For UEFA club competitions the corresponding UEFA regulations apply.

Article 76 Structure and Registration of Clubs

1. All football clubs, and sports clubs having a football branch, shall be registered with TFF in accordance with the terms of the 'Regulations on the Registration of Football Clubs' laid down by the Executive Committee of TFF.
2. (Amended by the decision of Congress at 01.06.2019) All football clubs, and sports clubs having a football branch, shall provide the TFF with their income and expense statements, balance sheets as well as their budgets for the next season and annual General Meeting minutes, as approved by their annual General Meeting, within thirty (30) days following the date of such General Meeting. If any club fails to fulfill this obligation or provides incomplete or misleading information in this respect, it shall be given a warning and the rights of its officials shall be suspended.
3. If the club fails to fulfill its said obligation within thirty (30) days from the date of the caution, then it shall be sanctioned with a deduction of points. If the club fails again to fulfill its said obligation within an additional period of thirty (30) days that will be given it, then it shall be relegated.

4. (Amended by the decision of Congress at 01.06.2019) The TFF shall be entitled to inspect any such financial statement provided by clubs. Any club which is found to be in the lack of financial strength required to meet its financial obligations shall be referred to the Disciplinary Committee and sanctioned with a warning, a fine, points reduction or relegation, depending on the gravity of the offence. The officials of the club shall also be suspended.
5. A club engaged in football may transfer its football branch to any joint-stock company established in accordance with the related laws and regulations. A club that has restructured itself into a business corporation may not transfer its registration to any other city.

   Promotion, strengthening and interests of the game of football shall be priority in such transfers.
6. No natural person or legal entity (including holding companies and subsidiaries) shall manage or have control over more than one club in any manner that would jeopardize the integrity of any match or competition.
7. The TFF Executive Committee sets up the corresponding regulations also covering fusion between two or more clubs, the transfer of headquarters as well as the change of name of clubs in the authority of the TFF.

VII INTERNATIONAL MATCHES AND COMPETITIONS

Article 77 International matches and competitions

1. The authority for organizing international competitions and organizations between National teams and between leagues or club teams belongs solely to FIFA and UEFA according to the appropriate provisions. No competition or organization shall take place without the prior permission of FIFA or UEFA.
2. The TFF shall comply with the international match calendar compiled by FIFA.

Article 78 Contacts

1. (Amended by the decision of Congress at 01.06.2019) The Club's affiliated with TFF shall not play matches or have sporting contacts with Associations or clubs that are not members of FIFA or provisional members of a Confederation without the prior approval of FIFA.
2. The same applies for suspended or expelled FIFA and UEFA members.

Article 79 Approval

(Amended by the decision of Congress at 01.06.2019) Clubs, or any other group of clubs that are affiliated to the TFF cannot belong to another Association or participate in competitions on the territory of another Association without the prior authorisation of the TFF, the other Association as well as FIFA and UEFA, except in exceptional circumstances.

VIII FINAL PROVISIONS

Article 80 Unforeseen contingencies and force majeure

1. The Executive Committee has the right to decide finally on any matters not provided in these Statutes or in cases of force majeure.
2. While taking its decision, TFF take into account of the FIFA and UEFA legislation and principles of truth and justice.

Article 81 Use of Facilities and Services of Staff

1. (Amended by the decision of Congress at 01.06.2019) The TFF may use, and allow clubs to use, sports facilities and services of staff members of the Ministry of Youth and Sports by signing an agreement and a protocol with the same for such purposes.
2. (Amended by the decision of Congress at 01.06.2019) The number of individuals who shall have access to the VIP stands of any sports facility which the Ministry of Youth and Sports has transferred or rented out to, or allocated for use for a limited time period by, sports clubs or public organisations or institutions under a protocol shall be decided by the related Provincial or District Directorate of Youth and Sports in line with the instructions of the Ministry of Youth and Sports and the VIP stands of such sports facility shall be organised by the same Provincial or District Directorate. In the event of an international representative match, the VIP stands shall be organised by the TFF in accordance with the related principles of FIFA and UEFA.
3. (Revoked by the decision of Congress at 12.6.2009).

Article 82 (Added by the decision of Congress at 12.6.2009) Leave

1. Any referee, representative, observer or a TFF Committee member, who holds a public office and is assigned to a match which will be played on a business or non-business day, shall be deemed to have official permission to be absent from his public duty throughout such assignment, provided that his supervisor has been informed thereof.
2. The time period of such assignment shall be fixed under the related regulations of the TFF.

Annex II

Article 83 Tax Exemption

Proceeds obtained from matches and competitions organised in Turkey under the control of FIFA, UEFA and the TFF and under this Law as well as all other revenues of the TFF shall be exempt from taxes, duties and charges of any nature.

Article 84 Entry into force

1. These Statutes were adopted at the Congress, which was held in Ankara on 03 June 2008 pursuant to paragraph f) of Article 2 of Law No. 3813 as amended by Law No. 5719, in accordance with the statutes, regulations and decisions of FIFA and UEFA and on the basis of the authority granted under paragraph c) of Article 6 of the same Law. However, the present Statutes shall come into force only if the law that will replace Law No. 3813 Concerning the Establishment and Duties of the Turkish Football Federation has been enacted by Parliament.
2. (Amended by the decision of Congress at 01.06.2019) The Statutes shall be published on the web site of the TFF (www.tff.org) in accordance with the decision of the Congress.

Article 85 Execution

This Statute is executed by the TFF.

IX TEMPORARY PROVISIONS

Article 86 Constitutional meeting for TFF Statutes and TFF Membership

1. The delegates present at the Congress in Ankara of 3 June 2008 participated at this constitutional meeting in which membership to TFF based on these TFF statutes was established.
2. This Congress was convoked according to the Law No. 3813 dated 17/06/1992 which was amended by the Law No. 5719 dated 04/12/2007.

Article 87 Terms of office of elected members of TFF organs and bodies

1. The TFF President, members of the TFF Executive Committee, the Auditing Committee, the legal committees under the previous Law. 3813 which was amended by the Law 5719 and who have been elected before 1st June 2008 shall continue their mandate until the term of office expires.
2. (Amended by the decision of Congress at 12.6.2009) However, members of the Referees' Committee, Committee Delegates and the other committees that should be established in accordance with the present Statutes shall be newly appointed by the TFF Executive Committee within forty-five (45) days after the coming into force of the present Statutes.

Article 88 Membership application

1. The participants of the TFF constitutional meeting of TFF in Ankara on 3 June 2008 are required to provide the TFF General Secretariat with all documents according to Article 11 of these Statutes within one (1) month following the enforcement date of these Statutes.

Annex II

Selected Bibliography

Aker, H. Futbol Karşılaşmalarına I lişkin Yayın Haklarının Hukuki Niteliği ve.

Atasü, T. & R. Güner. Türkiye Futbol Federasyonu Dopingle Mücadele.

Ayrancı, H. 'Sözleşme Kurma Zorunluluğu'. *Ankara Üniversitesi Hukuk Fakültesi Dergisi* (2003/1): 229–252.

Çalısşmaları, *Doping ve Futbolda Performans Arttırma Yöntemleri.* edited by T. Atasü, Ankara Türkiye Futbol Federasyonu, 2005.

Eren, F. *Borçlar Hukuku Genel Hükümler.* Ankara: Beta Basım Yayın, 2008.

Erkiner K. 'Türkiye'de Spor Hukuku'nun Oluşumu'. *Istanbul Barosu Dergisi Spor Hukuku Ozel Sayısı* 3 (2007): 17–40.

Erkiner, K. 'Dünyada ve Türkiye'de Sportif Yapılanması' *Spor Hukuku Dersleri* ed. K. Erkiner. Istanbul: Kadir Has Üniversitesi, 2007.

Ertas, S & Hasan Petek. *Spor Hukuku.* Ankara: Yetkin Yayınları, 2005.

Erten R. *Milletlerarası Özel Hukukta Spor.* Ankara: Adalet Yayınevi, 2007.

Genc, D.A. *Spor Hukuku.* Istanbul: Alfa Yayınları, 1998.

Guran, S. 'Turkish Administrative Law'. In *Introduction to Turkish Law*, edited by T. Ansay & D. Wallece, Jr. Ankara: Turhan Kitabevi, 2009.

Gürsoy, A. 'Professional Football Players' Contracts under Turkish Law'. *Ankara Bar Review* 1 (2008): 19–29.

Kızılot, S. *Gelir Vergisi Kanunu Uygulaması.* Ankara, 1989.

Kocasakal, U. 'Spor Hukukunun Özellikleri çervevesinde Tahkim Yargılaması ve Türkiye Futbol Federasyonu Tahkim Kurulu'. *Istanbul Barosu Dergisi Spor Hukuku Ozel Sayısı* 3 (2007): 41–56.

Ozbudun, E. 'Turkish Constitutional Law'. In *Introduction to Turkish Law*, edited by T. Ansay & D. Wallece, Jr. Ankara: Turhan Kitabevi, 2009.

Petek, H. *Profesyonel Futbolcu Sözleşmesi.* Ankara: Yetkin Yayınları, 2002.

Rekabet Hukuku Açısından Yayın Haklarının Merkezi Pazarlaması. *Ankara Üniversitesi Hukuk Fakültesi Dergisi* (2006): 1–46.

Yatkın, M.C. *Türkiye'de Sporcuların Vergilendirilmesi.* Ankara, 2006.

Law No. 2709. *Türkiye Cumhuriyeti Anayasası.* The Constitution of the Republic of Turkey.

Law No. 813. *Borçlar Kanunu.* Code of Obligations.

Law No. 4721. *Türk Medeni Kanunu.* Turkish Civil Code.

Law No. 6762. *Turkish Commercial Code.* Türk Ticaret Kanunu.

Law No. 4857. *Iş, Kanunu.* Labour Code.

Law No. 274. *Sendikalar Kanunu.* Union's Law.

Law No. 506. *Sosyal Sigortalar Kanunu.* Social Security Law.

Selected Bibliography

Law No. 193. *Gelir Vergisi Kanunu.* Income Tax Law.

Law No. 5520. *Kurumlar Vergisi Kanunu.* Corporate Tax Law.

Law No. 3065. *Katma Değer Vergisi Kanunu.* Value Added Tax Law.

Law No. 4054. *Rekabetin Korunması Hakkında Kanun.* Law of Protection of Competition.

Law No. 3289. *Gençlik Spor Genel Müdürlüğünün Teşkilat ve Görevleri Hakkında Kanun.* Law Regarding Organization and Duties of General Directorate of Youth and Sports.

Law No. 5894. *Türkiye Futbol Federasyonu Kuruluş, ve Görevleri Hakkında Kanun.*

Law on The Establishment and Duties of The Turkish Football Federation.

Law No. 6222. *Sporda şiddet ve Düzensizliğin Önlenmesine Dair Kanun* Law Regarding the Prevention of Violence and Disorderliness in Sports.

Law No. 3796. *İstanbul Kentinde Yapılacak Olimpiyat Oyunları Kanunu.* Law of Olympic Games which will be held in Istanbul City.

Decree Law No. 556. *Markaların Korunması Hakkında Kanun Hükmünde Kararname.*

Decree Law Pertaining to the Protection of Trademarks.

Decree Law No. 516. *Patent Hakkının Korunması Hakkında Kanun Hükmünde Kararname.* Decree Law Pertaining to the Protection of Patent Rights.

Decree Law No. 554. *Endüstriyel Tasarımların Korunması Hakkında Kanun Hükmünde Kararname.* Decree Law Pertaining to the Protection of Industrial Designs.

Decree Law No. 638. *Gençlik ve Spor Bakanlığı'nın Teşkilat ve Görevleri Hakkında Kanun Hükmünde Kararname.* Decree Law (Executive Order) Regarding the Organization and Duties of Ministry of Youth and Sports.

Index

The numbers here refer to paragraph numbers.